Transition Man

Transition Man

By

Jeffrey T. Mitchell, Ph.D., CCISM

And

William "Josey" L. Visnovske

Other books by the authors:

Crucial Moments in Time: Stories of Support in Times of Crisis (2015)

Sister Mary, the Baker, The Barber and the Bricklayer (2017)

Dedication

- Jeffrey T. Mitchell –

To Elijah John who dramatically changed lives before he was even born.

Love you, E.J.,

- Granddad, "Pop"

Dedication

- William "Josey" L. Visnovske –

I realize books are normally dedicated to those close to you, but this book is dedicated to an event. As hurricane Michael crawled over our home as a category three storm, I climbed the tree that threated to land on our roof. I knew, with each branch I grabbed, that this was a bad idea. At the top of the tree, I attached a chain and hand winched the falling tree to an Oak tree in our yard. There was a moment in the top of that tree where the world seemed to be calm and the balance of life was finally balanced. Hurricane Michael brought damage to our area, but what he left behind is why I dedicate this book to him. As hurricane Michael pushed on my family, we joined together and we pushed back. Every parent raises their children in hopes that they will be able to survive without them. I saw our boys as young men, clearing debris and helping others without being asked. Nor did they complain about being without power. My wife, who has watched me leave repeatedly to help others, was now the one who left to help others. Though hurricane Michel left us with his aftermath, he also gave us peace of mind that our boys have graduated from this part of life. As for that moment in the top of that tree, I guess that is between Michael and me.

Contents

NOTE: Josey's stories are all true. Comments by Jeffrey T. Mitchell have been added to many of Josey's stories. The commentaries enhance the meaning of the stories and add insights about recovery and healing. But some of the stories speak powerfully enough about recovery and healing on their own. Commentaries would add little to certain stories and were, therefore, not incorporated into the book. We hope for two goals with this book. The first is that you enjoy your reading and the second is that the stories and commentaries enhance your lives. Best regards from Josey and Jeff

Introduction

To me, the hardest part of writing a book is what to write for the sections called the Introduction and About the Author. I know they are important, but I write to process not promote. I also know that once you look at the front cover and turn to this section I have a limited time to grab your attention and make you read on. So, if my introduction reads like a short story that's because it is. It's a short story about a psychologist and a country boy who met and wrote a book together. The first book went over well so we did another with the added help of a paramedic that takes pictures to process. The psychologist, the country boy, the picture taking paramedic, and a city girl, who helps the country boy write better all wrote this book.

When I met Dr. Mitchell eight years ago, I had no idea that the introduction would take me down the path I am on now. To be honest, my life was simple. I was married, had two young boys, and a good job. Overall, I was blessed and happy. I had decided to do a specialty job within my own employment and that required me to do research. That research led me to a man I did not know and that man was Dr. Mitchell. At that time, Dr. Mitchell happened to be going through a divorce, an event that changed his life. I recalled our first meeting, where a boy who got his education on the dirt roads of America, was giving him advice.

Despite his concrete upbringing, it was not long before Dr. Mitchell became more than a research partner, but a friend. When Dr. Mitchell suggested that we write a book, I was reluctant, but he said a book would help people. Our first book was called *Crucial Moments, Stories of Support in Times of Crisis*. I did not help much with the book because the idea of people reading stories that I had written did not sit well with me. Those stories were my private thoughts that I had kept tucked away like a teenage girl who writes in her diary.

The feedback from book one was good so I decided that we should do a second book titled, **Sister Mary, the Baker, the Barber, and the Bricklayer.** My writing style had changed from the teenage girl who wrote in her diary to thoughts of people like you, who stand there and look into the sky, hoping to see a falling star. I wrote more for the reader and less for me. I wrote in hopes of bringing you peace, in hopes of learning from my failures, and in hopes of knowing that you are not alone in your thoughts when you're sitting on the sofa at 3 a.m.

Life is like a jigsaw puzzle where all the pieces don't fit together at first. We all suffer, we all have pain, we all bleed, and sometimes we struggle for our next breath. For example, I sat in a room the other day with 60 some odd people who do what I do and yet I felt alone. I questioned why I was there and for most of my life I have struggled to fit in and belong to something. I called a friend for guidance and she said, "In life we really only connect with five percent of society and your five percent is not there." After almost fifty years of living and trying to fit in, the answer was clear. My five percent are most likely the people who would read this book.

As I said earlier, my life was simple when I first met Dr. Mitchell, but in the last eight years it has been more complicated. Our partnership is good, and we are like two magnets stuck together, traveling down this path to help others. We have been blessed that other magnets have joined us and at times it feels like we are an unstoppable force. We continue down the path, but then we meet magnets that seem to have a different polarity than us, and that is where the conflict begins. That is where my life began to get complicated. Just when I was ready to close my diary pages to you and return to my simple life, I received an email from a man I had never met. A man who said that my written words had helped him to survive the loss of his wife and, four weeks later, the loss of his dog.

There is no growth without conflict so I decided to do book three. Dr. Mitchell said, "What's the theme of book three?" I guess this educated dirt road boy did not know that a book needed a theme, but I responded without hesitation, "Self-care." I dug deep into the diary box and pulled out stories from over 25 years ago when I wrote for me not you. I wanted you to see my need for self-care back then. I wanted you to see the path I was on. I wanted you to not make the same mistakes I did. I also dug into the diary box and chronologically walked the path to present day. You will see the change in the way I wrote for me versus the way I now write to you. You will see me get married, you will see the birth of my sons, and yes, you will see my growth with conflict. And so the puzzle pieces start to come together.

The pages will unfold with words and images in your head, but if that is not enough, one of the magnets that joined us will give you a picture to capture that moment in time. The stories are true, but I always left out the names and places ever since I started writing in the sixth grade. To me those details do not matter. What matters are the emotions that swirl around when the story unfolds in written form. Our hopes are that this book will teach you self-care and give you hope when you are searching the skies or feeling alone as you sit in a crowded room. We are simple people, who joined to write a book and possibly answer a few questions; maybe you can grow with us too. - **WLV-**

Story 1

The Specialist

As the alarm rang out, I rolled over and realized that I was not sleeping in a bed, but on a floor. I slept on the floor the first night in my new apartment as my coworkers weren't due to deliver my furniture to me for a few days. I made a pillow out of a towel and now the towel and I were headed to the shower.

I stepped outside and felt the cold north wind hit my face and my long, damp hair start to freeze. I realized that I had moved too far north for my liking. I passed a small grade school as I walked down the street that led to the college I was now attending. I heard the familiar sound of metal hitting metal. I turned to see where the sound was coming from and saw a brass buckle that was attached to a flagpole rope. The cold north wind was causing it to hit the flagpole. The sound reminded me of the flagpole at my little Catholic school, miles from this place. How I wished I were there instead of here. As I moved along the street, everything seemed to be frozen, until a mangy looking dog came running out from behind an old building, barking at me, but he was stopped short by the chain attached to his collar.

I managed to find my classroom and took a seat with the other students. I soon drifted off to a place that was far away from here, where I could hear nothing except the sound of water hitting the floor as my frozen hair thawed. I heard the instructor call someone's name several times, but the person did not respond. As she prepared to move on to the next student, I realized that the person's name she called was the name that I was using in this frozen land. I raised my hand and said, "Here." I knew from that point on that I had just committed myself to at least a year of being someone I was not.

This was to be my fourth long-term undercover investigation. This meant a year or more of living with the criminals in this town, having a job to blend in with them, and in this case, going to college with them. I had reached the point of being burnt out with the whole idea, but after this investigation I would be able to convert these college credits into my real name and use those credits to help me finish my four-year degree. It was a good deal, but I also know that every good deal has a hidden price, and this one was going to be the isolation from my fellow coworkers whom I had learned to rely on for pure sanity.

My furniture finally arrived, and I was able to sleep in a bed and have my own pillow. One of the first things I learned from one of my fellow coworkers was something he had told a criminal in a fit of rage. He said, "At least when I lay my head down on my pillow at night I can sleep because I know I am doing what is right!" I had come to realize that most things in life boil down to the pillow that we lay our heads on. As we rest, our subconscious takes over from where our conscious decided not to go, and from there we sort through our activities from the day. When I was here, I slept with a pistol under my pillow. I never knew when the criminal might find out who I really was and decide to come pay me a visit while I slept. My subconscious told me I was doing right, but sometimes, the fear of the criminal kept me awake.

As the first couple of months slowly passed, I found a job working in a bar. A bar was a good undercover job, but not for someone who was allergic to cigarette smoke. The cigarette smoke, the trips back to the last place I worked to testify in court, and going to school, compromised my immune system. I started to get a lot of allergy infections, so I went to see the

2

campus doctor. The campus doctor referred me to an allergy specialist in the town I was working, but I decided to try a specialist closer to my real home where I could use my real name and made an appointment. After several questions about my sexual preference and drug usage, the specialist said there was nothing he could do for me. I walked out with the feeling that the specialist did not want to treat me based on the way I looked. I didn't tell him what I did for a living, but I didn't think that should matter. I am the type of person that subscribes to doing unto others as you would have them do unto you, so I was disappointed that this specialist wouldn't treat me.

After that experience, I decided to try the specialist in the town where I was working. The specialist was a very tall man who was slumped over at the shoulders and had a very strange bedside manner. He reminded me of a scary person on the cartoon Scooby Doo. He very seldom made eye contact with me, but he did seem to listen to my every word. I could tell that he was in poor health. His eyes and face reminded me of an old dog that was falling asleep in front of a warm fireplace. After careful examination and no questions about my sexual preference or if I used drugs, he suggested I undergo testing to see what I was allergic to. My test results showed several allergies. The specialist made a serum and soon I was taking allergy shots to build up immunity to those allergies. Despite my long hair, beard and 6 earrings, the specialist treated me like everybody else. He had taken an oath to treat the sick. I was grateful that I found someone who would treat me even though that I looked like a criminal and was unable to reveal my true identity.

As the months pushed on I continued to fight the allergy infections and tried to continue with my love of exercising, the only thing that I believed kept me sane. My coworkers would call me, but it was not the same as seeing them. After six months of fighting the allergy infections, working long hours, and trying to tame the stress of pretending to be something I was not, the allergies took their toll. The specialist recommended admission to the hospital for a week to recover from this massive allergy infection and the other complications that arose from it. I refused him on Friday, but by Monday morning I was begging him to put me in the hospital.

I had never been in the hospital before so on my first visit, I just lay there with my head on the pillow and stared at the ceiling. I questioned my sanity since I allowed things to get this out of control. The specialist arranged for me to a have a private room. I tried to sleep, but it felt very unsafe here. After two days of no sleep, they realized it, and started to drug me so that I would sleep. As my subconscious took over, it too questioned if this investigation was worth me ending up in the hospital. Several times during these drugged states, I would awaken to find the specialist checking on me. When our eyes locked, he would turn and leave the room. I would look at the clock on the wall and at times it would tell me that it was the middle of the night. Though I looked like a criminal, it was refreshing, even if for a few brief moments, that someone treated me like I wasn't one. After five days, I was released. After that, I made sure to not run myself so far down that I would end up in the hospital again. I continued in the investigation and struggled every day to not just walk away. I had been dating a girl in a different place and she knew that I was a police officer. Sometimes, I would go and visit her, but even though my body was physically there, my mind was always at a different place. It was in that place where I lived my false life. While I was in the hospital, I decided to end the relationship with her and just concentrate on finishing this investigation.

I had learned to look forward to my visits with the specialist. He never said much, but he treated me like the person I was on the inside, not the person I appeared to be on the outside. Over the years, I had learned to accept that people will treat you this way, but it still does not make it any easier as it is happening to you. At around eight months, I started to crumble inside. My family and coworkers had no clue that this investigation was getting the best of me. The job had taught me how to disguise my true emotions, even from the good guys. I exercised more, but it did not help with the lonely feeling I felt inside. Even when I was around real friends and family, I felt alone. Most of all, I felt very cold. Like death had moved inside of me. I could no longer feel anything.

I realize now that my ability to keep things in order, even though I was falling apart on the inside, was, in part, because I did not drink any alcohol. I had seen what alcohol had done to others who had chosen this type of job and decided I would stay away from it. I had also seen what dating women inside the walls of the place you were working could do to negatively impact an investigation, so I never dated anyone on the inside. A coworker once said, "If you're not drinking all the alcohol and sleeping with all the women in the bars then you must be a cop." Based on that notion, I would occasionally have a female coworker come in and pretend to be my girlfriend so the women on the inside would think I had a girlfriend. This pretend girlfriend only added to the coldness that I felt. Almost everything in my life had become a lie.

I recall one night, which I believe was one of the lowest points of my time living with the criminals, where I was working in the bar and talking to one particular girl. She frequented the bar, but never drank much or went home with anybody. I knew she was not connected in any way with the people from whom I had been buying drugs. As far as I could tell the only reason she came to the bar was to dance. As we talked at the bar, she talked to me like I was a good guy and not the criminal that I appeared to be. As the conversation continued,

I began to feel very warm inside. I pondered this warmth and the next thing I knew, I asked her to go home with me. She asked why I wanted her to go home with me and I told her I just wanted to lie next to her. She laughed and left the bar. My answer was honest. I had no intentions of having sex with her; I just wanted to feel the warmth of another person. I never asked anyone to go home with me again.

A coworker used to say, "Working dope has peaks and valleys." By month 11, I had hit the bottom of this valley. The night was November 23 and I sat at my kitchen table for 4 hours and wrote about the last 11 months in this place. I read it now and weep with tears at the confused and cold person I had become. I had become a specialist. I was good at one thing, and one thing only, and that was being someone I wasn't.

As month 12 landed, so did an opportunity to end this investigation early and start a new one in a different place. At the new one, I would be able to go to college and in one more year I would graduate with a four-year degree. I agreed to the new assignment and looked forward to leaving this cold place. On one of my last days there, I visited the specialist. I asked the nurse to leave the room and told the specialist the truth about whom I really was. His tired eyes rolled toward me and for a few brief seconds he made eye contact with me. He said, "What can I do for you?" I replied, "I want you to continue to be my doctor, but it will be difficult because of my job." He said, "No problem, and put those scum in jail." He shook my hand and left the room.

Weeks later I returned to his office. By then, my 12 months of work had appeared in the newspaper and several people had been arrested. I was now a good guy to several people in his office who had previously treated me like a bad guy. From that point on, the specialist and I became friends. He was a man truly dedicated to his work. He had taken an oath and had taken it to heart. He spoke of a family, but I felt as though he saw them very little. He had another office that was located about 150 miles from his main office. Between two offices and his rounds at the hospital, it is no wonder he always looked tired.

My allergies improved when I moved away from that place, but once again I became consumed by my new investigation. I was closer to some of my coworkers and was also closer to family, so those things helped me get by. "Getting by" had become my way of making it day to day. The last investigation left me with a feeling that I was "damaged" goods. While I was effective at what I did, the isolation and the pitfalls that come with doing undercover work were taking their toll. I could see myself on the same path as the specialist and that scared me. Was I going to end up like him? I was thankful that after 12 months of hell I had at least had made a good friend out of it. I never met the specialist's family but had spoken to them on the phone. In a way, I had become the specialist's confidante. With me, he didn't try to hide or pretend to be someone he wasn't. If I needed a checkup, the specialist would meet me wherever to accommodate my schedule. No matter where my travels took me, I could always count on the specialist to call in a prescription for me. It was the perfect arrangement for a person who had two lives. It was also about this time that I was reunited with my first love and soon we had set a date to be married.

I finished my four-year degree and started applying for jobs with federal law enforcement agencies. Before long, I was flying to Washington DC to take some tests. I passed all of the tests, but one. I did not fast from eating before taking my blood test and because of that, it messed up the results. I was told to go to my own doctor and have the results sent in. The specialist took care of me and before long my days of having two lives were over. My wife and I moved to the East Coast and now I looked like everyone else. I had decided that the specialist would still be my doctor even though we were now almost 1000 miles apart.

When I would return home for court or to visit my family I would have the specialist give me a yearly checkup. It was when I moved to the East Coast that I believe our friendship really started to grow. It was difficult for me to speak to the specialist to talk over the phone. We agreed that writing letters was a good way to keep in touch. The specialist was a very intelligent man and his letters were sometimes difficult to read. I started to see where the specialist was trying to teach me not to make the same mistakes that he did. He would never come right out a say what the mistakes were, but if you read between the lines and his vast vocabulary, you could see and feel what he was trying to say. I would read certain sections of the letters to my wife to see if she could read between his lines and words, and she could.

In my new job I was no longer a specialist. In fact, I was like everyone else. When I was a specialist, I was good at one thing and terrible at everything else. Now I had the opportunity to be good at a lot of things. I felt sorry for the specialist because he never had the chance to be good at anything else. He had made himself into a great doctor, but in every other area he was extremely insufficient. Our letters continued, and with each passing one, I started to have a greater understanding of the man who first reminded me of that scary person on Scooby Doo.

Over the next few years, I switched jobs a couple of times, searching for my niche in life. The specialist never said much about my job changes, but he did say that he was very much against me living with criminals. In the spring of one year, I landed the job that I always wanted. The specialist was very happy for me and sent a letter stating that. About that time, a friend of mine died and I wrote a story about him. I mailed it to the specialist and he told me that he was really moved by the story. The specialist had sold one of his practices and moved to a nice lake resort. It seemed that the specialist and I had finally found our peace.

I was out at my adopted Grandfather's farm one weekend, playing with my German shepherd and shooting some handguns, when I received a page. I looked down at my pager and saw the number. It was the specialist's home number. When I got home I called his number and his daughter answered. I asked for her father and she said, "I have to tell you something." Before she could say the words, I already knew what she was going to say. The specialist had died of a heart attack at the age of 54. I'm not sure how I knew, but I knew. I was in the middle of mandatory training for my new job but felt that attending his memorial service was just as important as my new job.

After talking with his daughter and wife, we agreed that I would give the eulogy. I wasn't sure what I was going to say, but I had kept several of his letters. Inside those letters was what I felt that he wanted to tell the world but could only tell me. My wife and I went to the service, which was 1000 miles away. As I walked down the hill to the outside chapel, I asked the preacher to point out the specialist's wife. It seemed strange that I was giving the eulogy because I had no idea what his family looked like. Minutes later, I was face to face with the wife, daughter, and two sons of the specialist. They were glad to finally put a face with the voice that they had heard about for 6 years. My heart was beating very fast as my wife and I took our seats. Even though this was no dope deal, my blood pressure was climbing rapidly. I carried two guns that day, one for me and one for the specialist. Like me, he was a firearms enthusiast and always enjoyed seeing new guns. The time came for me to address the crowd of people and shed the tears that I had been fighting back. I stood in front of complete strangers and wept. As I pulled myself together, I managed to make them laugh and cry. I held a letter the specialist had written to me and read these words:

"Each of us has to find the right place for us to be relative to our physical abilities, our emotional needs and emotional reserves, the needs of our family for our time, the needs of our family relative to worrying about the risks of whatever we are doing in general as well as the effects on our minds and bodies from the workload we are undertaking, etc. Every thinking man who cares has to find the right balance between his need to have positive affirmation that he is making a positive and unique contribution to his society as well as taking care of the needs of his family as well as not letting work take life's enjoyments from him. Those who dedicate themselves 100% to work as I did for almost 20 years miss out on the absolute priceless time that we have on earth that should reasonably be used to "smell the roses" and get some true enjoyment out of life."

If the specialist were here today that is what he would say to this crowd. I told the family, in front of the crowd, that the loyalty I had for the specialist was now passed down to them. When I finished, the crowd stood and clapped.

My wife and I went to the specialist's house where I was examined by many of his friends and family. Unlike an examination by the specialist, most of this was done from across the room. His wife intrigued me; she was not what I expected. As my wife and I left that evening, I noticed a certain look in the eyes of the specialist's wife. It was not the look of a grieving widow, but more of a look of curiosity for what I knew. As we drove back to our home, the miles of highway gave me plenty of time to reflect. I reread the letters in my head and attempted to see if I had missed something. I had my suspicions that the specialist might have been having an affair but was never sure. After I looked into the eyes of his wife, I was sure my suspicions were right.

I started to email his wife and before long she told me what she wanted to tell me the night we left. In their 20 years of marriage he had three affairs. When he sold the one practice and moved to the lake resort it was supposed to be a fresh new start. While his wife was cleaning out his office she found evidence that he had never stopped. My friend and specialist was a terrible father and husband, but a great doctor. His wife was now a grieving angry widow. I attempted to comfort her, but I myself was struggling with thoughts of how a man who was such a great doctor could also be such a flawed person. It wasn't long before I started to see the similarities between myself, when I lived with criminals, and the specialist in his own life.

I continued with the training that my new job required. When I was off on the weekends, I would try and sort through the confused feelings I had for the specialist. I felt like the criminals must have felt when they discovered that their friend (me) was really a police officer, and now they were going to jail. I wasn't going to jail, but when I laid my head down on my pillow at night, my conscious and subconscious fought for the time that was set aside for sleep.

A few months after his death, I bought one of his rifles that he had purchased for deer hunting. The specialist had many weapons that he planned to use for hunting, but he never took the time off to go. In the early morning hours, I killed a deer with one of those rifles. As I stood over the dead deer, I wondered if the specialist was proud of me. In the 6 years of living with criminals, I had stopped hunting, fishing, and everything I enjoyed. All I did was buy dope and pretend to be

11

someone I was not. I continued to stand there and think about the letters that he wrote to me. I thought about the things he tried to tell me. Most of all, I thought about his oath that he took to heal the sick. I recalled the audience at his eulogy and how most of the people there were patients, not friends. As the thoughts raced through my head, and as the last of the blood drained out of the deer, I started to cry, not for the deer, but for the specialist.

Based on how I knew him personally and through the letters, it was difficult to reconcile how such a brilliant and gifted human being could put himself on a one-way course for disaster. He was nothing more than a falling star; bright and full of life, but he knew it would only last for so long. He even realized the failures of his ways, but felt it was too late to start over. I recalled how he was so against me living with criminals and now it was very clear to me why. He knew I would become like him, a specialist, who might not be able to find the strength to turn around and return home. I grabbed the deer and dragged him back to my Jeep, leaving a trail of blood and tears behind.

As I write this story, it has been a year since the specialist died. In that year, I learned to move on with my life. I emailed his wife every day and we usually talked once a week on the phone. She too learned to move on with her life. In a sense, I became her confidante too. In me, she confided the mixed emotions that she has for the specialist, but to the outside world she is still just a grieving widow. Like me, she and her children sorted through those mixed feelings that some people leave us with, and the damage that life's situations can bestow upon us. I carry a great deal of respect for his wife. She took an oath and took it to heart, "till death do us part." Everything in life takes work. It's tough and it's gritty. It leaves marks and scars, but eventually we heal. Self-care and the choices we make, to do the work or not to do the work, greatly impacts our lives and who we are as people. It reminds me of a song by Montgomery Gentry called Tattoos and Scars:

> "…You see what these are, just my ragged old and jagged ordinary scars. He said, I got this one in Paris, in war 'fore you were born. And this one when I was half your age workin' on Daddy's farm. And you know the way I see it, son you ain't seen what I've seen, Cause tattoos and scars are different things. He said, I've been here all these years, and what I know is this, if you look and listen close, A man will show you what he is. You know the way I see it, you've been round, but you're still green, Cause tattoos and scars are different things…"

It also became clear to me that, besides the pillow we lay our heads down on at night, life also boils down to the oath we take, and how we honor it. Five days after the one-year anniversary of the specialist's death, my wife and I celebrated five years of marriage. When I took the oath of marriage, to me, it was the same as taking the oath to be a police officer. My father always said, "If you're going to do it, do it right. Do your part." For me, that meant twenty-four hours a day, seven days a week. When I took the oath of marriage, it was difficult, at first, to honor my oath to my wife, and my oath to my job. The first couple of years of marriage, I must admit, the job took priority over the marriage.

Between the letters from the specialist and the death of a few significant friends, I started to see the wayward path I was on. When I landed in my current position, I feared the waiting for that position would cause me to become consumed by the desire of wanting it for so long. I see now that the untimely death of the specialist sent a clear message to me. I am now better able to balance and honor both oaths. When people first get married, I know it's not one's intention to be unfaithful to their spouse, but after five years of marriage, I think I can now

13

understand why some people might find it difficult. I can also now understand, after 10 years of law enforcement, why some police officers may find it difficult to stay motivated to be the best officer they can be when the system beats you down. I say I can understand it, because I too have struggled to find that balance. It would have been easier to continue down that wayward path, but I decided that being unfaithful or allowing the job to consume me was not an option and never would be.

There are times that I reflect on how nice it would be to go some place and pretend I am someone else; to forget about the troubles of my life and to create a make-believe world that I could escape to. That is how I see the failures of the specialist; he felt he could not go home and face those who knew him best, so he would find those who knew him not at all. To those people, he would say what they wanted to hear, and for a short while he would escape his real life. I guess the specialist and I had more in common than I thought. In a sense we both worked undercover, but for many different internal reasons. We both used the excuse of our jobs to protect us from having to deal with the reality of home. We both justified our actions because of the needs of our society. We both lived two lives and we both lied.

The clock on the wall tells me it is time to go to bed. I take a final look at the picture of the specialist that I have hanging on the wall and turn out the light. Things have changed. I'm no longer isolated, I lay next to my wife, my first love, a woman who loves and accepts me for who I am, failures and all, and I no longer sleep with my gun under my pillow. As I drift off, my conscious takes a break and my subconscious takes over. There I will visit my friends who have moved on, died, or have forgotten their way home. As I fall deeper into my subconscious, I pray that wherever the specialist is, he has finally found his peace. I thank him for showing me the way to the roses.

14

Jeff Mitchell & Wm. Josey Visnovske

In memory of The Specialist: 1945-1999.

Written by a patient and friend.

Footnote: at the request of the specialist's widow, I laid his ashes to rest in the ocean with a single rose, read his quote, and cried.

- WLV-

The Actor's Price

Actors, industrial spies, CIA and military operatives, undercover federal law enforcement agents, police investigators, and just about anyone who lives a secret double life for a prolonged time is vulnerable to certain types of dangerous and destructive distress. Undercover stress syndrome can change personalities and it may cause some people to become solidified into the false roles from which they may find it extremely difficult to withdraw. Some require psychotherapy to recover from the split in their lives. Having lived a lie for so long, they may find themselves lying about almost everything. Some go as far as to violate their moral code and engage in criminal acts well beyond their legitimate law enforcement mission. Others withdraw from social contact. Relationships and marital problems are quite common among people who lead secret lives in addition to their 'normal' lives. Still others get physically sick and some develop serious mental problems. A few have serious psychiatric breakdowns that required prolonged psychiatric hospitalization. These are the unexpected consequences of undercover work. They are the actor's price. (John Violanti, Research Professor of Epidemiology and Environmental Health, University of Buffalo, School of Public Health and Health Professions, Expert in police stress).

Josey came dangerously close to crossing some clear and some poorly defined lines. In either case, had he done so, there may have been some very negative life-altering consequences. The signs and symptoms were very real and very obvious. They may not have been so obvious to Josey who was enmeshed in his perilous undercover work. In his state of mind at that time, he would have had a difficult time recognizing his isolation and nostalgia for earlier, happier times in his life as a symptom of his internal conflict. He wished to be almost anywhere else

16

than where he was at the time. He was distracted and disengaged, the very mental conditions that he could not afford because they made him more vulnerable to the real threats to his life. People who want to stay alive cannot be distracted and inattentive especially when working undercover. He had thoughts that bordered on paranoia, although they could be justified by the real dangers he was in on an almost daily basis. He lived in a state of elevated fear. He was sleep deprived, angry, resentful, and he felt emotionally cold. He was not in good psychological shape nor was he in good physical shape.

His body was in full-blown rebellion against his split between his two opposing lives. His work caused his allergies to tobacco smoke and other substances to join the body's rebellion. There is a saying in the field of psychology and it reads like this: "The body keeps score." Josey eventually figured this out when he ended up in a hospital for nearly a week. He had become a specialist in being someone he really wasn't and his body and mind did not like his specialty one bit.

Sometimes it takes a specialist to heal a specialist. Josey was fortunate to connect with a physician who respected him and was willing to work with him despite the difficulties associated with Josey's job. They became friends – good friends. Josey needed a trust worthy friend specialist far more than he needed a physician who specialized in allergies. Their friendship grew stronger and it was one of the important influences that helped Josey let go of the life of the undercover officer and change jobs several times to ones that caused far less physical strain and destructive emotional distress.

Josey's friendship with the Specialist came to an abrupt but honorable end. Josey then acted on the respect and appreciation he had gained for his Specialist friend and offered emotional support to the Specialist's loved ones for some time after the Specialist's death. The friendship was so valuable to

17

the young undercover officer that Josey was, he could not just let the friendship die. He offered admirable care to the Specialist family and provided an invaluable communications link to the Specialist's wife until her life could stabilize. It was just one specialist helping another to the very end.

- JTM -

Jeff Mitchell & Wm. Josey Visnovske

Story 2

The Marathon

During hay season, my best friend Dan and I worked for a local farmer named Bill. Bill was married but did not have any kids. His farm was our playground as kids, and one of our favorite places to hunt deer and turkey. Everything on Bill's farm had a name. There was Bill's Trash Dump, Bill's Bluff, Bill's Salt Lick, Bill's Bottoms and Bill's Hog Pen. Bill's father was a farmer and so was his father. Bill raised chickens, and he would go to town once a week and sell the eggs, but that was the only business he did off the farm. One time, as Dan and I walked through Bill's Bottoms, we decided to build a fire before we climbed the hill to Dan's house. In the far distance, we could hear our high dollar coon dog treeing another mouse. Dan and I had bought the coon dog with money we made putting up hay on other people's farms, but I don't think the dog ever treed anything but mice. We gathered up half frozen broom sage and started a fire. We warmed our young bodies next to the fire and watched the smoke roll out of Bill's Bottoms.

We knew it was late and decided to put the fire out and head home because our moms would be worried. We climbed the long hill that left Bill's Bottoms and connected to Dan's family farm. As we walked through the pasture, I could see a porch light on at Dan's house. I said good-bye to Dan and walked his gravel driveway that connected to the county gravel road. As I walked down the road, I decided to take a short cut through the woods to my house. I was halfway to my house when my flashlight died, but there was enough moonlight, and I knew the woods well enough, to find my way home. I walked into the house, and my mom met me in the kitchen and asked if we had any luck. I said no, and headed upstairs to bed.

Every year, my wife and I have a small family New Year's Eve party for our friends. My wife makes her famous deer chili, and we have a few finger foods. The party starts at dark, but ends a few hours later because the next day is an important hunting day for me. As I attempted to light the fire for the party, I could not help but think back to that night with Dan 30 years ago. Every time I light a fire, that memory returns.

I finally got the fire started as our friends arrived. As I served the chili, I looked around at who showed up this year. There was Al, my friend who owns a feed store; Richard, who works for John Deere; Cooter, who works on my Jeeps; and Chris, who is a local farmer who helped me out one day. The kids were throwing sticks into the fire, while the rest of us just sat around and enjoyed the night's air. My 20-month old son crawled up onto my lap, and my mind drifted back to Bill's Bottoms. I thought about Dan and how I missed those days. I held my son and smiled at my wife who was sitting across from me. There are only two things I like about being an adult; being married to my wife and having a son. As the evening wound down, we made some to-go containers of my wife's chili and said good-bye to our friends. My wife took our son inside to get him ready for bed and I cleaned up the remnants of the party.

At 4 a.m. my alarm went off. I got up, fed my dog, and fixed myself two biscuits. The mother of a friend of mine makes me homemade biscuits that I eat for breakfast and snack on during my twelve-hour deer hunts. I packed my backpack with biscuits, trail mix, protein bars, and water. The baby monitor told me that my son was awake. I looked at my watch, it was 5 a.m., and he was on schedule. My wife leaves for work at six, so we get up early in our house. I walked back to my son's door, and with my dog following me I rushed into the room and yelled "police with a search warrant!" He jumped up in his crib laughing, with his favorite blanket in hand. I picked him up and took him to the kitchen where he had some milk and a banana. After he finished his breakfast, we got a clean diaper and played on the floor for a few minutes. I looked at my watch. It was 5:30 and time for me to head to the woods. I told my son it was time to wake up mama, so we walked back to the bedroom door, and ran in and yelled, "police with a search warrant!"

My wife asked where I would be that day, and I responded in the swamp. She smiled and said, "Swamp yoga, be careful." My wife calls it "swamp yoga" because, sometimes, when I come home from work, I'm really frustrated with the world we live in, and she will tell me to go to the swamp and clear my head.

My dog and I went out to my shop where I loaded her into her crate. My dog does not hunt deer, but she has been trained to track a wounded deer. I started up my old Jeep and drove about a mile to my buddy's farm. My friend owns a large farm that belonged to his father and his father before him. I have a choice of hunting in the woods, fields, or the swamp. By far, the swamp is my favorite place to hunt. I drove back through the field and parked my Jeep. In the back of my Jeep, I have four different rifles to choose from. I picked the one that is my favorite. I put on my backpack, shouldered my rifle, touched my dog's nose, and headed for the swamp. It's about a mile walk to the swamp. I could have driven closer or have gotten even closer than that with a four-wheeler, but I feel we humans have made roads into places that we should have left alone. I worked my way through the swamp and found the tree where my stand is strapped some 30 feet off the ground. I climbed the tree, pulled up my rifle, clipped my safety harness into the tree, and hung my backpack on a hook. The platform of my stand is not much bigger than a truck floor mat, and the seat is about as big as two egg cartons sitting side by side. I got settled in for my 12-hour day and waited for the sunrise.

One of my favorite times of the day happened 30 minutes later. As the sun started to rise, I could hear the ducks on the swamp flying out to the different ponds and creeks. I heard the turkeys calling to each other and then all of the other unknown birds started to sing. The creek that runs through the swamp made its own special sound from the rain we had the day before. Our deer season is four months long, if you include bow season. I bow hunt, muzzleloader hunt, and rifle hunt. I fill our four freezers within the first months of deer season with deer meat (there is no such thing as venison in my house). After our freezers are filled, I spend the rest of the season just watching the deer and processing the previous eight months of my life.

Most people spend New Year's Day eating chips and dip, cleaning up chips and dip, or saying that it will be the last chips and dip they will ever eat. New Year's Day has become a special day for me in that I spend the whole day in the woods. I think about the year gone by, how I could do things differently, and those days in Bill's Bottoms. The swamp, to me, is holy ground, a place where there is little human sign. When I'm in the swamp, I try really hard not to even leave a footprint in the mud. There are some old stumps from trees that were logged years ago and occasionally, a tin can will float down the creek. I guess, to most people, the swamp is a nasty place. The mosquitoes are almost as big as birds. I've had a few water moccasins coil up on me, but I never shot them because, the way I see it, I'm a guest in their house. I almost drowned in the creek a few years ago while tracking a wounded deer, but even after all of that, I still love the swamp. This deer season, I took time off from work to do nothing except hunt the last three weeks of the season. My wife knew that I had been working through some problems and that maybe three weeks in the woods would help me find some answers.

I graduated from junior college with a degree in criminal justice when I was 21 years old. I had decided to sit out a semester before transferring to a four-year college. I spent some of that time building fences for Leroy, a local farmer who had worked the farm handed down to him by his father. And just like the land owned by Bill, our previous employer, Leroy's land had similar distinctions; Leroy's Bottoms, Leroy's Pig Pen and so on. I was building a fence on a hill that overlooked much of Leroy's farm.

One day after working, I received a phone call about going to work as an undercover police officer. I took the job and over the next six years, I pretended to be something I wasn't, and was good at it. It was an unusual job that took a certain type of person, and I was that person. After six years, I thought that if I could do this much good at the local level of law enforcement then I could surely do more if I went into federal law enforcement. I have been working at the federal level for ten years now and the days that I dislike my job far outnumber the days that I love it. As far as my personal life goes, I have the perfect family and a great circle of friends. I have changed jobs a couple of times within the federal system, and have moved several times, but I'm still unhappy. I thought maybe three weeks in the woods might shed some light on my unhappiness or at least give me three weeks away from work.

I reflected back to 1999 when a friend of mine had died. Years before his death, he wrote me a letter. In that letter, there was a paragraph that has haunted me everyday since his death. He had written about the balance we need in life and how he had struggled to find it his whole life. My friend was a doctor and was much smarter than I ever will be. I know if he would have told me in person, I would have understood what he was trying to tell me, but in his written words, it was over my head. One of the rifles I have to choose from when I hunt belonged to him. It was his favorite rifle, he had plans to take it out west and kill "the big one," but he never even fired the rifle. After his wife gave it to me, I had a friend change the stock and scope and work on the action. It was a high dollar rifle and now I wanted to finish what he had started. Every time I hunted that season, I would look at the rifle, but never take it. I wanted to save it for "the big one" or a doe at 500 yards. I knew, with only two weeks left in this season, I would have to use it sooner or later.

The perfect day for me is to wake up next to my wife, wake up my son, get a kiss from my dog, watch the sun rise, and sit in the swamp. So, I decided to head to the swamp to clear my head. At noon, I reached into my backpack and ate two biscuits. A pair of Otters swam down the creek, but there were no deer. As fast as the sun came up, it set over the swamp. I could hear the ducks flying into the swamp like fighter jets landing on an aircraft carrier. In the distance, an owl hooted, and that told me it was time to leave that place that I love and go home to see the other two things that I love. Using God's natural light, I packed up my gear, climbed down from the tree, and walked back to my Jeep. As I walked up to my Jeep, my dog stuck her nose up to the crate door to smell my hands for deer. She didn't smell anything, and I told her, not this time. I drove home, parked my Jeep in the shop, went into the garage, pulled off my boots, and walked into the house just in time to kiss my little man on the forehead, and tell him goodnight. My wife asked me if I had a good day and I told her yes. After showering, I lay down and was asleep within minutes after my head hit the pillow.

The next day, I returned to the woods. When faced with the choice of rifles, I chose the doctor's and hunted a ridge that overlooked the swamp. I sat there, holding the doctor's rifle, and tried to figure out what I should kill with it. A nice 8-point came by a few hours later, but I did not shoot him. After ten hours in the stand, I decided to hunt the last two hours in one of the fields. I crawled back into some brush along the field and went prone with the doctor's rifle. I had my high dollar scope zeroed at 300 yards and knew that I could accurately shoot out to 600 yards. I watched a group of does come out into the field, but did not take a shot. As the sun set, I eased back into the brush and went home.

When I got home, I told my wife that my neck and left shoulder really hurt. She asked what I had done, and I told her about hunting in a prone position out in the field. She suggested that I might want to take a break. That was her way of telling me that I was overdoing it. When deer season starts, I usually hunt a few hours before work and all day Saturday and Sunday for four months. When deer season is over, I'm usually sick, have pulled muscles, and have lost about 10 pounds of muscle from not eating adequately. A lot of people hunt to take a break from the wife and kids. Some want to bond with their buddies and talk about the girls they dated in high school, and some hunt for the horns or for the meat. Then there are those, like me, that hunt for answers.

The days that followed New Year's Day were special days. I was privileged to watch a lot of deer. When I was younger, I just killed the deer and seldom took the time to just watch them. I envy deer in how simple their lives are. They only need three things; food, water, and a safe place to sleep. My wife is the closest human being I know to being a deer. Her needs are minimal; a roof over her head, a modest car to drive, and a job. Somewhere in the process of becoming an adult, I got lost, and think that it takes six Jeeps, four rifles, and multiples of everything else to make me happy. My wife, by far, is the most balanced person I know.

One day, I decided to hunt over one of my food plots that sat below a pond dam. I have several food plots on my friend's farm and I also have seven deer feeders that I run all year. I see the deer as a herd of cattle; if I take care of them, they will take care of me. My father always said that the earth was not ours; "Whatever we take from her, we should give something back in return." Shortly after dawn, a pair of raccoons came up under my stand, and I fed them my morning bag of trail mix. They saw me sitting up there, but were just happy to be fed fruit and nuts. One even put his paws on the small ladder that is strapped to the tree and acted like he was going to climb up. I was only able to stay in the stand for about 6 hours before my shoulder and neck started to hurt so badly that I felt I wouldn't be able to take an accurate shot at a deer.

I got down out of the tree and did some sneaking around. When Dan and I were younger, we called it "super sneak mode." I think hunters from the city call it stalking. I hunted a different field that night and watched a 6-point buck and a doe come out into the field. It was clear by their body language that they were a couple. I sat next to a tree, but my shoulder and my swollen tonsils were really hurting. A few months ago, an ear, nose, and throat doctor figured out that I kept having sinus infections because my tonsils were bad. He wanted to remove them, but I told him it would have to wait until deer season was over. I went home that night, walked into the house, and lay down on the kitchen floor. I told my wife my shoulder was killing me so she got out her medical books, and after reading, she felt I had strained a muscle in my neck that was causing referred pain in my shoulder. She thought it was from all the hours sitting in the tree and lying prone in the field. She showed me how to massage it and told me to ice it when I could. She never once said to stop hunting. I realized at that point that I would be unable to shoot prone because of the pain, so I had to come up with a shooting platform for my field hunting. I went out to my shop and grabbed an old lawn chair that sat close to the ground. I sat in it with my head lying against the back of the chair and my arms on the armrest; there was no pain. I placed a milk crate in front of the lawn chair and put my backpack on top of it. I then placed my rifle on the backpack and sat in the chair. I slid out of the chair and sat down in front of the rifle. I pulled the rifle to my shoulder and looked through the scope. I had a little pain, but not as bad as lying prone. I took the lawn chair and milk crate outside and spray painted them green.

I went to bed that night with an ice pack on that muscle in my neck. A few hours after I went to bed, I woke up, and felt like someone had stuck an ice pick in my shoulder. I went out to the living room and put more ice on it, but could not get any relief. My wife got her medical books out again and read that lying in a bed could make the pain worse, but lying in an elevated position could help it feel better. We had a rocker/recliner easy chair that I never cared much for, but my wife used to rock our son in it at night. My father was not one to sit around in an easy chair either, and I'm the same way. However, I thought the chair might allow me to get some sleep. In a few hours it was 4 a.m., and I was back in the woods.

I hunted in three different stands that day. It was hard to sit for very long without the pain getting worse. I massaged the little muscle and did a neck stretch that my wife suggested. I knew with only a week left in the season, I needed to kill something with the doctor's rifle. I kept waiting for the perfect deer, or for that really long shot, but nothing seemed to be right. In this particular tree, my stand is 40 feet off the ground. I sat there and thought about the doctor and his life. I wondered if I had become like the doctor. I had hunted so hard that I exhausted a muscle in my neck. My tonsils were swollen and infected, but

I still managed to hunt. The doctor spoke of balance and by far, I was about as unbalanced as they come.

I thought about my job and how I disliked it. Being a police officer or soldier, one must come to terms with the fact that you could die doing your job. One would think that if you were willing to risk your life for your job, then it would only make sense that you must love your job or the cause. When I was a local police officer working undercover, I would have been honored to give my life for that cause. I think my wife was the only person that understood why I joined the Marine Corps Reserves at the age of 33. I just felt like I was not doing enough for society in my current job. I know that anybody could do what I do now, and the cause seems to get lost in all the red tape, forms, and memos.

I sat there, 40 feet in the air, and decided that whatever came up the draw this evening, it would go home with me, and I would spend the next day with my son. About an hour before sunset, a doe came up the draw; she was only 75 yards away. I raised the doctor's rifle and put the cross hairs on her. I released the safety and squeezed the trigger. She never knew what hit her. She was not 500 yards away and she was not "the big one," but she was a deer, and I had managed to do more than the doctor had. I climbed down from the tree, walked over to the doe, and called my wife to tell her I would be later than normal. I field dressed the deer, walked back to my Jeep, and called the doctor's wife to tell her I had killed a deer with his rifle. When she asked how big and how far he was, I said he was a she, and it was only 75 yards. I explained my decision to just shoot something, and that maybe it was one of the things that he tried to tell me in that letter. I told her that I hoped he was happy wherever he was.

When I got to my Jeep, and put my hand to the crate door, my dog's tail wagged so hard it thumped in the crate. I unloaded

my dog and let her track the deer even though I knew where
the deer had finally laid down. Then, I loaded the deer and
drove home. I backed up to my deer-cleaning shed and my
wife brought the little man out for his good night kiss. I told
her that there would be no day care the next day because the
little man would spend the day with his daddy. The next
morning, I woke my son in the usual fashion, but instead of
wanting to play on the floor, he sat between my legs with his
blanket in one hand and two fingers from the other hand in his
mouth. There was no TV, no toys -- he just sat between my
legs.

My shoulder and neck still hurt and my tonsils were still
swollen. I was sleeping full time in the easy chair and every
morning I remembered the sensation of ice picks from the
night before. Despite the discomfort, I took my painted lawn
chair and milk crate, and headed for one of the fields the next
morning. I trimmed a small opening in some brush and made a
place for my gear at the edge of the field. I almost felt guilty
for having such a comfortable set up. I thought for a minute
that I might have become a city hunter, but none of them
would have painted a lawn chair over ordering something out
of a catalog. As the sun rose, I'm aware that I never cease to be
amazed at the beauty. I don't find much beauty in things that
man has made, but what God has created is truly a gift that
most of us take for granted. I spent most of the morning in my
painted lawn chair and never saw a deer, but that was okay. At
noon, I ate my two biscuits and did some sneaking in the
swamp. Three hours before sunset, I headed back to the field
and sat in my lawn chair. I never miss a week in the woods
because I plant my food plots, fill my feeders, keep the coyote
population down, and watch the deer throughout the year. But,
this was the last evening of deer season and the reality that it
was the end of the season was setting in. Turkey season would

be here in a few months, but it would be another 8 months before deer season would be back.

About 15 minutes before sunset, three mature does came out into the field. I slid down from my lawn chair and sat behind my milk crate. I pulled the rifle to my shoulder and looked through the scope. They were exactly 300 yards away. I still had room in my freezers, and I could always use more meat. I placed the top cross hair on the biggest doe and released the safety. As I moved my finger onto the trigger, I took a deep breath and then released it. Then I put the safety back on and sat up. Sometimes it's not about killing the deer, but about watching them. So, I stood looking at them as they grazed peacefully in the field. I started to pack up my gear, took a minute to breathe the night air, watched the deer one last time, and enjoyed that moment, because I have learned that things change.

The last time I was in Missouri, I was not allowed to hunt on Bill's farm. A few years ago Bill's wife died and some distant relatives moved Bill into their home. Bill lived for several more years, but recently died, and now his relatives own the farm. Last deer season in Missouri, I hunted next to Bill's farm where they had logged, cut down, and bull dozed just about everything you can think of. Cedar thickets that were a place for deer to rest and turkeys to roost are gone forever. We humans call it progress.

I packed up my gear, grabbed my lawn chair and milk crate, and eased back into the woods. It was quicker to go through the field, but I did not want to interrupt the grazing does. As I cut through the woods to my Jeep, I passed the stand where the raccoons ate my trail mix. I walked up to my Jeep, and my dog put her nose up to the crate door and smelled my hand. I said not this time -- maybe next season. I drove home and parked my Jeep in my shop. As I reached to turn out the light in my shop, I saw a note taped to the wall that my wife had left for me at the beginning of deer season. It said, "Congratu-ulations on your first deer of the season, I love you, I'm going to bed." I walked into the garage, opened the door into the house to tell my wife that I was home, and there stood my little man. I don't know if it was a surprise or on purpose, but the little man was behind schedule. He reached up for me to pick him up, so I did. Then, then I took him out to the garage where he helped me take off my boots, my safety harness, and all my other gear. He put on my lucky hat that a friend had given to me after his tour in Operation Desert Storm. On the front of the hat is my Marine Corps Eagle, Globe and Anchor pin that I received on the parade deck at Parris Island. On one side of the hat is a small rubber alligator that my wife gave me. I looked at my little man and thought about the doe that I almost shot, and had I shot her, I would have missed out on these few special minutes with him. I took him into the house, got him ready for bed, gave him his bedtime snack, brushed his teeth, and placed him in his crib. He lay there with his blanket in one hand and those two fingers in his mouth. I told him I loved him and that we would be hitting his door at 5 a.m. with a search warrant. My wife was getting ready for bed as I undressed to take a shower. She said she was sorry that deer season was over. I told her it was okay because it would be turkey season in a few months, and I laughed.

By the time I got out of the shower, everyone was asleep. My dog was sleeping on a pad on the floor at the foot of the bed, and I could tell she was worn out. I walked into the room we call our office. It has our computer, a whole wall full of framed pictures, and a shelf full of memories. I sat down at the computer to check the weather and realized it did not matter which way the wind blows tomorrow—deer season was over. I turned around in the chair and looked at the wall behind me. I saw pictures of Dan and me as kids with deer and turkeys;

Dan and me as adults with deer and turkeys; my dog and me with deer and turkeys; and the most current one was of me with my son outside of the hospital where he was born. I focused in on a picture of the doctor and read the printed words that were inside the glass. Each of us has to find the right place for us to be, relative to our physical abilities, our emotional needs and emotional reserves, the needs of our family for our time, the needs of our family relative to worrying about the risks of whatever we are doing in general, as well as the affects on our minds and bodies from the workload we are undertaking. Every thinking man who cares has to find the right balance between his need to have positive affirmation that he is making a positive and unique contribution to his society as well as taking care of the needs of his family as well as not letting work take life's enjoyments from him. Those who dedicate themselves 100% to work as I did for almost 20 years miss out on the absolute priceless time that we have on earth that should reasonably be used to "smell the roses" and get some true enjoyment out of life. As I read his words, tears rolled down my face, and I once again asked him what he was trying to tell me in that letter.

I thought about my job and how much I dislike it, but who would like a job where 80% of your time is behind a computer and the other 20% is dealing with some of the nastiest people society has to offer? I thought about how all the red tape drives me crazy, but as my boss says, it would drive me crazy to work for any major organization. That was his way of saying I'm a country boy.

I sat there and looked at all the pictures on the wall. All the pictures were of me hunting, being a country boy, or being with good friends and family. I focused in on the picture of my wife and me standing on the parade deck at Parris Island, and I was smiling. I looked down at the shelf under the pictures and saw the wooden box that had held the remains of the doctor. A few months ago, at the request of his wife, I took him to the ocean and set him free. I walked out to the garage and stuck my hand in the pocket of my hunting pants and pulled out tree bark, protein bar wrappers, and one shell casing from the doctor's rifle that killed the deer. I walked back into our office and put the spent shell casing into an old military mess kit that Dan and I had used when we camped as kids. Also inside the mess kit was a knife that my wife had given to me for an anniversary gift one year. I used that knife to clean a turkey, and three days later, my wife's doctor let me use it to cut my son's umbilical cord. The knife is now retired.

I sat back in the chair and realized that very few people knew much about the doctor's personal life. For the most part, he did not have one; he was just a doctor. I asked myself if I would want to be remembered as a special agent or as a husband, father, friend, and hunter?

I thought about my New Year's Eve party and how no one there was connected with my work. I thought about how no one from my work has ever been to my house. There were no pictures of work stuff hanging on this wall. Then I realized that for ten years I have struggled with being unhappy in my job, even though both my job and my title have changed several times. As a federal agent, I swore to an oath, and I carry a badge and a gun, but my heart is still that of a small county deputy buying drugs on some dirt road, without the aid of paperwork, surveillance, or red tape. When I was in local law enforcement, the job defined who I was, now it's just what I do. I would want to be remembered as the man that hangs on this wall, not the man that carries the badge. I'm proud to be a husband who truly loves his wife, a father who carried his young son in a back pack so he could experience nature, a friend who was loyal, a man who joined the Marine Corps at age 33, a deputy that served society, and a hunter who just loved being in the woods. As the tears rolled down my face,

35

the four months of mental and physical exhaustion set in. I looked at the doctor's picture and told him that maybe we humans get balance and happiness confused---that maybe it's hard to find happiness when we are out of balance.

I turned out the light and headed for the now familiar easy chair. The house was quiet, except for the dishwasher running in the kitchen. Every muscle in my body hurt. My shoulder and neck were killing me and it hurt to swallow. I eased the chair back and the night light across the room illuminated a deer mount that I had killed on Bill's farm. Some people call them trophies, but to me it was a living memory of my life. I looked at the deer and thought back to the morning I shot it. I thought about how Dan helped me drag it out and how his two kids helped me process it later that night. I thought about the small wood stove burning in his garage and how his kids felt like big people helping us cut up the deer. I thought about how Bill's wife would cook huge lunches for us, when we were kids, on the days we would put up hay. I thought about how Bill would let us cool down in his basement and give us a sip of his homemade raisin jack wine. To me, it's not a trophy, but a part of my life that I cherish as much as the birth of my son; it's who I am. I came from the hills of Bill's farm, Leroy's Bottoms, and all those places that many deer and turkey have called home. My dog walked into the room and lay down next to the easy chair. The only sound I could hear was her breathing. I closed my eyes and filled my head with the memories. I took a deep breath; the four-month marathon was over. I thanked God for what met me at the finish line; my loving wife and son, freezers full of deer meat, and memories that will carry me for years to come. Memories that will sustain me on the days when the world makes no sense and as I struggle to find balance, or is it happiness?

****

Jeff Mitchell & Wm. Josey Visnovske

This story was written in memory of farmer Bill, Leroy, Dan, his brothers, his father, my friend's farm that I hunt on now, and all other farmers who do what they do; not for the money, but for the love of the land. They farm the land like their fathers did and unlike my job, it's who they are. I thank you for giving me a place to make memories.

On February 11th, following the marathon deer season, our 12-year-old German Shepherd, died as she had lived; with a brave heart, and a loyal and devoted spirit. There will be more hunting seasons, more times in the swamp and the woods, but there will always be a missing piece. In my constant quest for answers and understanding, I realize that her devotion and unconditional love will always be with me to soften my view of the sometimes-harsh realities of life.

"Until one has loved an animal, part of their soul remains un-awakened." -Author unknown.

- WLV -

A Place to Process

"Death is either an incredible ending to a story or more often than not, if you ask the right questions, it is the beginning of a story." – Alex Graves - University of Toronto

In the story of the Specialist (Story One), Josey's physician and good friend died of a heart attack. A few years passed and Josey had not fully processed or "come to terms" with the loss. He had questions and concerns that still needed some work. Grief is like that. It doesn't just fade away because a certain amount of time has passed. It takes time and it takes a little mental work.

It really helps if a person has a place of peace, solitude, quiet and comfort. It is a safe place where someone can work through their private thoughts and their personal issues. For some it is a room in their home like a bedroom, a workshop, a garage or a basement. Others prefer a church or a park or the seashore or a hiking trail.

Josey has such a place and it is the swamp where he hunts. It is the place where he can think, sort things out, make plans, and appreciate nature and the good things of his life. It is a safe place for him where he can process losses; find solutions to problems and answers to questions. It is a place where he can write his stories in his mind.

Josey entered the swamp in this story with four rifles, a back-pack with food, ammunition, ropes, tools, and clothing items he might need. Josey goes in prepared for marathon hunting sessions where the days can last twelve hours or more for three to four months at a time. These necessities were not the only things he brought to the swamp. Josey entered the swamp with a large imaginary bag filled to the top with memories, feelings, thoughts and experiences. He would sort through his imaginary bag and complete, simplify and categorize its contents. All the work in the imaginary bag doesn't always get completed during a hunting marathon but as Plato, the famous ancient Greek Philosopher once said, "The beginning is the most important part of the work."

Some people would assume that if a hunter saw a deer in his gun sights that he would pull the trigger. Not Josey. He did not always pull the trigger. He only took an animal when he needed it for food for his family. The killing of another creature had to be the right thing for him. It had to feel just right to him or it would not do it. In this story he used the rifle that was once his doctor friend's. The doctor had died before he had a chance to use that rifle. Josey did not hunt, like many do, for the pleasure of the sport. He hunted to feed his family or to hone his skills. In this case, he shot the deer to honor the memory of his good friend. Sometimes he just enjoyed the sight of the deer and its presence in nature. He often hunted to focus his thinking or to process some personal thoughts.

In the "Marathon" he reviewed old ideas and found some new ones in his imaginary bag that answered some of his questions or gave him greater insights into his world. He found some meaning in the letters written to him by his doctor friend, the Specialist.

- JTM -

Marine PFC Zachary Boland

Story 3

The Rubble of Life

Dear Nathaniel,

By now you have figured out that I'm a no show on this day. Please let me explain, but first, you have to follow my instructions to a 'T'. Move away from the crowd. Take a knee. I know you got tired of hearing take a knee. Once your knee is on the parade deck, feel the asphalt on your knee. Look around and see the new family you have, plus the family that you already had. Take a deep breath and smell the good and the bad of the island. Listen hard to every sound around you and recall the sounds that you recorded while on this sacred ground.

I had every intention of being there, but my boys really wanted to see their Aunt that is dying in north Missouri.—the same one who wrote to you. My boys are on Thanksgiving break this week, so I had to make a decision. I also thought about how this day is about you and your family and how my boys and I may distract from that moment. I'm sorry, but my heart is with you now.

I must confess, writing letters to you was probably more for me than for you. When I learned of the boy who picked up his brother's rifle after he died at boot camp, I was moved in a way that I needed. You see Nathaniel, I struggle with the hope that our younger generations can keep the pace that some of us have chosen. I have seen the rubble of life, I have seen the darkness of night on the brightest days, I have felt pain and suffering, and stood as a player and witness to this. The story of Zach and Nathaniel gave me hope that our younger boys can and will keep the pace. You could have hated the Corps, but instead you embraced the Corps. You could have spent the rest of your life questioning why, but instead you picked up Zach's rifle and said, "I am a witness and now I want to be a player."

We all came to the island for various reasons. I'm pretty sure, at my late age, I came to the island because of the rubble of life. I'm pretty sure, it too was the rubble of life that brought you to the island at your young age. Most Marines find the rubble of life after they leave the island. When you leave the island, you will have left a part of you as we all did, but you will take more with you than just the clothes that were on your back. You will take what all of those before you gave as they stood on those gold footprints and did their best to fill the shoes of those before them. No matter what rubbles you find yourself in from the battlefield, your backyard, the streets or the dirt roads, no one can ever reach so deep inside of you to take what the island gave you. You, my brother, are now a United States Marine.

As for the Ka-Bar, the best gift a man can give to another man is a knife or gun. You can display it or use it. I'd use it. If you get the blade dirty from blood you can wash it off. Bottom line, it's a tool to get you home. It's a tool to remind you of this moment in time because there will be days when the rubble is tall. Take a knee to remember my words and where this journey began.

Stand up Marine; the world awaits you. Thank you for inspiring me to push on. Thank you for that double dose of hope. Thank you for picking up Zach's rifle and embracing the Corps.

Josey

Note: This letter to Nathaniel Boland is included in the book as a tribute to the Boland family. Marine PFC Zachary Boland, the second oldest of 6 Boland children, was 18 years of age when he died from complications of pneumonia during boot camp at Parris Island, South Carolina, on November 4, 2016. Zachary had dreamed of being a Marine since he was 11 years old. One year later, Zachary's brother, Nathaniel, the third oldest of the 6 Boland children, also joined the Marine Corps to fulfill his same dream. In spite of Zachary's untimely death and the grief that the Boland family endured when Zachary died, Nathaniel was determined to become a Marine no matter what. On November 22, 2017, Nathaniel completed boot camp, and his dream, at Parris Island, joining the ranks of his brother Zachary and all those who came and served before them.

After I learned about the Boland family's story, I was inspired to write letters to Nathaniel while Nathaniel was in boot camp. Their story reminded me of a piece I had written about the back pocket dreams that most of us die with. We either don't get the support to follow our dreams or our plans change. When I joined the Marine Corps at the age of 33, many told me I was crazy. I guess, as a married man, who had a four-year degree and a good job, people would question why I would enlist in the Marine Corps to become a ground-pounding Marine. To me, it made perfect sense; it was a dream and I wanted to better serve my country. So, when I heard the story of two brothers who had become Marines, where one died trying and the other did not back down from his dream, I knew the time had come for me to support a young man who was a much younger version of me. Writing letters to Nathaniel was the least I could do to support him, the Boland family, and the memory of Zachary Boland. Semper Fi.

https://www.washingtonpost.com/news/checkpoint/wp/2017/0 5/24/their-son-died-at-marine-corps-boot-camp-now-they- have-a-message-for-other- recruits/?noredirect=on&utm_term=.1e5bbf3248a7

- WLV-

Jeff Mitchell & Wm. Josey Visnovske

45

Story 4

The Curtain

It's 3:58 a.m. and my alarm will go off in two minutes. I've been lying here for over 30 minutes trying to go back to sleep, but no such luck. I could hear my wife breathing because she was still getting over the cold that she caught from one of the boys. I could also smell the subtle fragrance of her shampoo that lingered around her head like a crown. Even though my body called for sleep, my mind remembered a time when I lived at a bar and the only thing I could smell was my own smoke soaked hair from living undercover. Moments like these make me feel privileged to love and have the love of a good woman.

Today is the last day of our five-month deer season. As I lay there, I tried to figure out where I should spend the last day of season. I hunt deer in much the same way that other people approach life. Some people go to see a movie and sit up front where it feels like the actors can reach out and touch them. Then, you have those who sit in the middle of the crowd, to blend in and feel like they are a part of it, but the actors would have to jump out to touch them. Then, you have the ones who sit in the back where the actors can barely see them and would never know if they left.

At 5:00 a.m., bowling ball number one came down the alley with two fingers in his mouth and his blue blanket dragging behind him. He climbed up onto the dog crate that sits under our kitchen bar and used the roof of the crate as a bar stool; his day has begun. A few minutes later, bowling ball number two came down the alley with his thumb in his mouth and his white blanket dragging behind him. I picked him up and put him in his high chair; his day has begun.

At 6:00 a.m., the queen of the bowling alley came down the hallway and informed the balls that they had two minutes to "saddle up." By 6:05 a.m., the balls were loaded into the car. Off they went to daycare, and the queen rolled on to her day job. Before the taillights faded from my eyesight, I was standing in front of my footlocker pulling out my pine scented hunting clothes. By 6:30 a.m., I parked my Jeep on my friend's farm and walked to my stand. On the weekends, I'm normally in the stand by 6:00 a.m., but age and memory have taught me the importance of being present for the little moments, like waiting for the bowling balls to come down the alley. By 6:45 a.m., I was in the tree with my rifle, bow, and camera. I chose a stand where I was sitting up front, so close, that I'm hesitant to move my leg, for fear the deer will see my movement.

The last day of deer season is always the same in my mind. I relive the last five months and try to sort through the things that troubled me during the seven months that led up to deer season. I also try to figure out how I can be a better person by contemplating the steps I need to take to ensure that I balance my love of family and my love of these woods.

We teach our children to put away their toys and that lesson continues on into adulthood. The problem I have discovered is that there are some things we encounter in life where there is no toy box to put them in. There are things that trouble the mind and things that we know are wrong, but they still happen. Some things can scar us more on the inside than the outside. Then there are things that we see, smell, hear, feel and remember. Some of these things try to come home to our bowling alley. I come here to these woods to try and find a home for these things, to try and find a toy box to put them in.

I can see the ground now. It's a cold day, but the sun will make it warmer. Once this season, I was able to take my three and half year-old son hunting, our first hunt together. I have always known that most behavior is learned. I've seen it first hand in my many years of being a peacekeeper in law enforcement. My oldest has been coming to the woods with me since he was six weeks old, but he had never been deer hunting. As we walked to the ground hunting blind, he knew to whisper and followed my every footstep. I leaned over to show him a deer track. When he asked what the other track was, I said, "A daddy track." I told him that all of God's creatures make tracks, even us. He sat quietly in the hunting blind and waited for the deer. After I shot a doe, he whispered, "You got him." I showed him the doe and explained that we were going to walk the same path back to the Jeep and then return to get the doe. He had a puzzled look on his face about the word path. I explained that some people call it a road or a trail, but it can also be called a path. I told him that all of God's creatures follow a path, a road or a trail. I placed him on my shoulders as we walked back to the Jeep in the dark. He never said a word until we got home and then he told his mom all about his first hunt. I was amazed at how he knew how to behave while we hunted. Then I realized that he had been watching hunting videos and me.

It's now 2:00 p.m. and for a fleeting moment, I saw the hooves and lower legs of a deer in the brush about 40 yards from my tree stand. The brush is very thick in here, much like smoke in a bar. In less than four hours the season will be over and my mind has so much more to sort through in preparation for the next seven months.

Every day I see how the ill intentions of one dark soul can affect many others for years to come. For example, the other day, I sat in a room for hours with a man who had been traumatized in his youth. Since he was able to run along in life without falling or having a course correction, he, in turn, has traumatized many people in our society. It's days like those that constantly remind me that many people think only about themselves and forget about everyone else in our society.

I sat in a lot of trees over the last few years and realized that the roots underneath the soil all intertwine, much like us. It does not matter if you are rich or poor. We all breathe the same air, drive the same roads, drink the same water, and sit on a toilet.

The job of a peacekeeper is to keep the peace. After 19 years of being a peacekeeper, I am told that I should be bitter, sarcastic, and without hope. Why? Because in part the job of peacekeeper takes its toll. However, the more time I spend keeping the peace, the more I realize that I am just a paper towel trying to soak up those "things" that we really don't know what to do with. The real job of keeping the peace falls on all of us. It could be the way we speak to the clerk at the grocery store or the way we speak to the stranger who is trying to help you fix our computer. It could also be the way you act in front of your children. Being kind can breed kindness.

It's now 5:00 p.m. and I'm tucked back into some brush, watching the field, waiting for the last act. I continually looked through my binoculars, waiting for the white-tailed deer to appear for their final performance. Thirty minutes before dark, I spotted the ears of a doe standing at the edge of the field. She scanned the field for predators and told the fawn next to her to wait. God designed a deer with predators in mind; eyes on the sides of their head, ears with the ability to turn in every direction, noses sharper than a dog's, and that gut instinct that humans, for the most part, tend to ignore. Then, the doe signaled to the fawn, that it was okay. The fawn bolted out into the field like a child in a parking lot. The doe ran behind it to protect it from the predators. I envy the doe. She does not have to worry about the drunk who just left the bar, the drug dealer selling crack on the corner or those who, like some serpents, camouflage themselves as your friendly neighbor down the road; the one who looks like us, smells like us and goes to church like us. He could be a friend, a teacher, or a family member. The list is endless. The doe only worries about the predators that God put on the earth to balance the herd. As the curtain falls on this performance, I look at my watch and see that it's over. The season has come and gone like the first steps my boys took.

I packed up my gear, slipped back into the brush, and followed a trail to my Jeep. I know this trail and have used it for years. I don't need a flashlight; I trust my memory. My backpack feels 30 pounds heavier than it did at the start of season and I'm tired. As I walked in the dark, I wished that more people would realize how we all follow trails. We all make tracks and we all sit in the audience. I also wished that more people would be careful with the types of tracks they leave behind. We should take notice that all of our trails are connected and that where you sit in the audience affects us all. Our number one oath, before all others, is to protect our little ones, our fawns, and our bowling balls.

In a few days, I will return to these woods and remove my 20 deer stands. The only sign that I was here are a few tracks and smashed down brush from where I dragged a deer or hog out. The kind of sign that a few rains and a change of season will erase. The other thing I leave behind are those "things" that man has created, those "things" that man does not know what to do with. I leave them hanging on tree limbs, in the brush on the ground, unseen to the naked eye, but I know they are there. I hope and pray that Mother Nature will filter those "things" back into the soil so they never trouble another person.

Transition Man

I came down the trail. My Jeep was a welcomed sight. I was tired. As I began to remove my backpack, I heard a faint whisper above my head, "Daddy, the deer sleeping?" "Yes baby, the deer are sleeping."

- WLV -

Jeff Mitchell & Wm. Josey Visnovske

Toy Boxes

"We're so used to everything being properly manicured, like you can hear every footstep in a movie, you can hear every bit of dialogue, and everything is in its place." - Jon Brion - American composer and song writer

The human brain is a marvelous and astonishing organ that sets the human being apart as the most extraordinary creature on earth. The brain houses the human's mechanisms for complex thought, information processing, memory generation and storage. Among innumerable capabilities, the human brain analyzes, synthesizes, deconstructs, shuffles, reconstructs, develops ideas, plans, decides, dreams, problem solves, remembers, and regulates the body's vast array of physical functions. The human brain houses the components of the human system that generate, control, remembers, and communicates emotions. It is a common belief that the human soul, the spiritual core of human being, is housed within the brain.

To some degree, "The Curtain" is a story about the human brain. It suggests, for instance, what the human brain always attempts to do is to learn, interpret, and store a massive amount of information from an astounding assortment of sources. There are three things the human brain is especially adept at doing. The brain always attempts to complete every experience it encounters. It is not a hundred percent successful, but it will always try to complete things. The brain does not like unfinished business. Like in a "who-done-it" movie, the brain searchers out clues. It tries to solve mysteries. It tries to help you figure out the ending before you get to the ending. It tries to finish a story, solve a mystery, complete a building or a bridge under construction or make sense out of a tragedy.

In addition to attempting to complete the experiences it encounters through the senses, the brain works toward simplification. The brain may be the most highly complex organ in the world, but it specializes in making things simple so we can manage them. The brain develops formulas and memory joggers and fast-track pathways to conclusions. The brain likes short cuts. Again, it is not always successful and it can misinterpret things and sometimes make mistakes, but the brain is a master of simplifying things and that is generally a good thing. Simplification helps us to deal with some of the complexities of life.

The brain is a champion when it comes to categorization. Benjamin Franklin often said, "A place for everything and everything in its place." The brain always tries to put things in their own place in its memory systems. It makes it easier for us to retrieve memories when they are organized into categories in our brains. We might think of the brain's memory storage system as a great many little boxes in which most of the elements of a specific memory are stored. Josey refers to them as "toy boxes" in his story, "The Curtain." Sometimes several boxes have to be opened up to bring a memory into our consciousness or to solve a problem. Those would be the associated memories that are stored in their own boxes. When put together, associated memories help to complete our thoughts and to figure out what we need to do. They guide our behaviors and our interactions with others.

Some memories don't fit in with our other memory boxes. Traumatic memories are a good example. So are evil things that happen in our lives. The brain has trouble sorting out where those memories belong. Those memories are dis-connected from all of our other memories. The brain, the intellect and the emotions haven't yet come to terms with them. They are called "disassociated" memories. They can make us uncomfortable and distressed. Sometime dissociated memories can cause us great emotional and even physical pain. Dissociated memories get put into a kind of unlabeled and broken dissociated memory box with a jumble of other dissociated memories. They may remain dissociated for a very long time until we are able to come to terms with them. In some cases, dissociated memories are of the evil things and we may never be able to associate them with our normal memories. They were traumatic when they occurred. They can remain traumatic irritants throughout our lives. We may not be able to find peace with them.

Josey talks about those memories (the dissociated type) that don't seem to have a box or they get put into an unlabeled "In-Box" with all of the other dissociated memories and unsolved mysteries of our lives. They tend to keep recycling over and over. We work on them for a bit, but we can't seem to get them sorted out so they go back into the In-box. One thing is certain. If we don't bring them out ourselves, they tend to find a way to the surface when we least expect them. Many years after a traumatic or evil event occurred, dissociated memories nag at us and demand our attention even when we would rather think of other things.

Josey leaves his dissociated memories in the swamp. They are not visible to others. He hopes Mother Nature will absorb them and make them disappear so that they don't harm other people. He knows, however, that those disturbing dissociated memories will still be there when he comes back to the swamp for another round of head clearing. Sometimes he will come to terms with one of these dissociated memories or a mystery will be solved and he can then associate those completed and categorized memories within his associated memory system and within the context of his life.

- JTM -

Story 5

The Yellow Bus

As I pushed the door open to the small, roadside, country store, I felt as though I was stepping back in time some 50 years. The floor was uneven, but the smell of home cooked food overloaded my senses and the floor seemed to even out. I headed towards the food counter and made eye contact with an older woman who reminded me of many of the farmers' wives I knew as a child. Her skin was weathered from working in the fields and the knuckles of her hands told me she had held many a field hoe. I asked if she had any gravy to go with those biscuits, but she replied 'no'. I could tell her answer bothered her, she had helped many a lost soul with the taste of her food.

I heard a familiar voice and it was the man who owned the roadside country store. His name is Mark. I met Mark several years ago when my well broke. We had a mutual friend who had called Mark when my well broke and he fixed it. My friend told me that Mark had worked as a well driller, a mechanic, a truck driver and anything else he could do to pay the bills. Mark fixed my well that day and was gone before I could thank him.

After that day, I made a few inquiries about Mark. I was told his father was a difficult man and his mother was a hard-working woman. I was told that Mark married young and had one son, but divorced soon after the boy was born. Mark married a second woman who had two sons from a previous relationship, but she died in his arms on the side of the road a few years ago. Mark adopted, in his heart, not legally, her two sons, and was now married to another woman who helped him raise the two sons he adopted.

I was told by several people that Mark was a little on the wild side. Not the kind of wild that causes people pain, but the kind of wild that makes one think that in order to enjoy life you must be at "full throttle." I could relate. I heard that Mark opened the country store because it was a dream of his. Before the invasion of gas station convenience stores, many families supported themselves on these roadside country stores. Stores that catered to the famers and workers who worked in the fields, but times have changed.

I walked over, said hi to Mark, asked how business was and as always, he said, "Fine." I soon learned that the older woman behind the food counter was Mark's mother. I asked her if she could make me gravy to go with the biscuits and she said, 'Yes.' Later, I would call her before I went down to the store and she would make me a special batch of gravy to go with the biscuits. Mark did his best to keep the store open, but times have changed, and he was eventually forced to close the store. Now that the store was closed, I asked Mark's mom if she would make me biscuits that I could cook at home. She agreed, but I said, "I would prefer they be whole wheat biscuits." She told me that it would take some time to figure out the recipe, but she would let me know. A few weeks later, I received a phone call from Mark's mom and she said, "Come pick up your biscuits."

Mark's mom lived down the road from the country store in a small brick house that had belonged to her mother. The house was simple and the yard was clean. I walked up on the back porch and knocked on the sliding glass door. She was sitting at the kitchen table and motioned for me to come in. I sat down at the table and she explained that the whole-wheat biscuits were a "work in progress," but the first batch was ready to be tried out. I sat there for a half an hour talking about life, her kids, her grandkids, and then in the middle of a sentence, she stood up and removed the biscuits from the freezer and placed them on the table. She sat back down in her chair and looked at me. I asked her what I should call her and she replied, "Granny Hilda." When I stood up to leave, she hugged me and told me she loved me.

There were many batches of whole-wheat biscuits made before she felt the recipe had been perfected. I averaged two whole-wheat biscuits a day so Granny Hilda knew when it was time to make more biscuits for me. As the years passed us by, I became friends with her son. Sometimes I felt like just one more stray dog that Mark had dragged home to his momma's house. I enjoyed my biscuit pickups from Granny Hilda's house. We would sit and talk about life and where we were headed. Occasionally I would show up in a new Jeep and she would ask me if Mark liked it. I told her that Mark loved it. He wanted to put Life Flight on standby, get a 12 pack of beer, and head to the river. Granny Hilda would look me in the eye, as she reached over and put her weathered hand on mine, and say, "Don't let Mark drive." I often viewed Granny Hilda as a mother hen tending to her flock. Her flock was her own children, her grandchildren, anyone who followed Mark home, and anyone who walked inside her yard. She was a sweet loving woman.

You could tell that with one wing she would protect you but, if you needed it, her other wing would knock you down. Granny Hilda's house was also known to host a few parties. She even had an out building set up with an outdoor kitchen and pool table.

Before I knew it, I was sitting at Granny Hilda's table telling her that my wife and I were having a baby. A face that was wrinkled and tired came to life, as she was so happy for me. My son soon learned where Granny Hilda kept the toys in the back bedroom and my biscuit picking up time also became playtime for my son. Granny Hilda would tell me which toys her kids loved and which toys her grand kids loved. None of the toys required batteries and could be sold on eBay as collectables.

As the years moved forward, Granny Hilda's health moved backwards. I noticed a decline in her breathing and she moved slower. She told me that she was getting her affairs in order and was giving things to her kids, so she could see them smile. I soon found myself at her table telling her that my wife and I were having another baby. Once again, her tired face and eyes came to life. My second son soon learned of the bedroom where the collectable toys were kept.

Mark and Granny Hilda always made it a point to invite us to all the family functions. I was never sure if they felt sorry for us, because our families were 1000 miles away, or if they really enjoyed our company. Granny Hilda always gave me a detailed list of who was going to be there and would tell me every time, "Just come and eat." Mark and Granny Hilda both knew I was not big on crowds and more than about four people was a crowd to me.

Mark soon became Uncle Mark to my boys and Granny Hilda was the house with the toys and biscuits. A few weeks ago, Granny Hilda's health took a turn for the worse and gave all of us a wake-up call that her days were numbered. Her family was having an annual get together at her house and my family was invited. I wasn't sure that I wanted to go and be around people because we had just received some disturbing news about a close family friend. In the end, I decided that being around some good people might take my mind off my own troubles. As my boys ran and played with the other kids I watched several people visit with Granny Hilda as she sat on the back porch where it looked as if she was sitting on a roost. She had a long tube of oxygen being pumped into her lungs from the house, but it did not seem to bother her. I found myself on the back porch telling her of my troubles and she listened with her tired eyes showing the pain she was in. She never complained about the pain, but I could tell she was tired. The kids had moved into the house and were playing with the collectable toys. My youngest son decided to turn off her oxygen machine, but she never complained about his actions.

The annual get together lasted two days. Over those two days, I met Granny Hilda's oldest son who had moved off to the place with streetlights and billboards. Granny Hilda's daughter, who had graduated from law school, was also there, but only lived a few hours away. Granny Hilda's daughter was a younger image of herself. Her name was Luanne. Luanne was very much like Mark and had his intensity for life. I did not see her having the "full throttle" lifestyle, but you could

61

tell she had plenty of fire in her. I observed this about her after one of the relatives had lost a small ball in a brush pile located behind Granny Hilda's house. No matter what the occasion is, a true redneck will find a way to use his truck or tractor at the drop of a hat. So, Mark fired his tractor up, and with my oldest son sitting on his lap, he pushed the brush pile over. As we searched for the missing ball, the only woman that entered where the dirt and broken limbs were, was Luanne. She picked up an old field hoe and started to use it to move the dirt around. I watched her hands as they wrapped around the old worn handle and for a moment I was looking at a younger version of Granny Hilda. As people continued to eat and talk of times gone by, I saw Granny Hilda's oldest son grab his camera and take a few pictures of his mother on the back porch. I could relate with his actions; I too was a son that had moved away. No one said a word about Granny Hilda's days being numbered, but it was clear to me that she was an active participant in her own living visitation.

A few weeks later, Mark called his mom one morning, but she did not answer the phone. Mark drove from work and found his mom had passed on. I had heard the news from a friend and called Mark. I could tell he was upset, but like always he remained strong. I asked Mark if the 10-minute ride from his work to his momma's house was a long one and he said, "There was a certain calmness to it." The following day, Mark called me and asked me if I would say a few words at his mother's gravesite and I said 'Sure.' Granny Hilda did not want a funeral with all the bells and whistles, just a drop off at the cemetery. Simple - Granny Hilda style. The cemetery was located just down the road from where Granny Hilda was born, raised and died. I imagined that Mark may have hid from the police, at this same cemetery, on one of his attempts to out run them back when he lived life at "full throttle".

I stood in front of the crowd of people and told them I would not tell them what a great person Granny Hilda was. If they thought, she was a bad person they would not be here today. I told them of how we met and how I became one more chicken that she tended to. As I tried to hold back the tears, I attempted to explain to them the person she was and what she stood for. I also pointed out that, in her opinion, her life was easy, but to the rest of us, it was hard. I also said that we are blessed to have people like her because no matter how much pain they are in; they can still feel our pain. I finally explained to them that I believe we are here to do a job, not a job that pays the bills, but a job to better our society. Maybe Granny Hilda's job was to raise her children or the children who found themselves in her yard or the adult who missed the taste of home cooked food. We will never know what Granny Hilda's job was, but she did it good, never complained, and did it with little to work with. Whatever Granny Hilda's job was it was finished and it was time for her to go. There is nothing that we can say or do to ease our sadness when someone has finished their job here. We can talk of the after world, quote scriptures, and say she is no longer in pain, but the bottom line is that we miss her. She left behind children that have the same fire as her and, just like she did, they will make the best of what they have.

Mark invited me to come back to Granny Hilda's house and eat with friends and family. I would normally hesitate, but not today, I wanted to go. As we drove up to Granny Hilda's house most everything looked normal. There were people standing in the yard eating and talking. We entered Granny Hilda's house and that is when it hit me. A dessert table replaced the kitchen table and the house was full of people I did not know. My oldest son, not missing a beat, entered the bedroom and found the collectable toys. He rolled a yellow school bus out into the living room and hit a few people in the legs. I saw a few people look down at him with disgust, but I knew Granny Hilda would approve of his actions. My oldest son soon found other kids to play with and left the yellow bus on the floor. My youngest son took over pushing the yellow bus across the floor and received some of the same looks. Luanne was in the kitchen being a young version of her mom. Her legs were stronger than her moms, but she had the same wings as her mom. The refrigerator was still covered with dozens of pictures of "what matters" and even had a picture of my boys. I soon found myself lost in the moment and realized Granny Hilda was not here in body, but her spirit was present. My youngest son continued to push the yellow bus around as Luanne tended to her flock. I looked out the window and saw Mark talking to people and he too was tending to his flock. I stepped off the back porch and watched the children playing in the yard and felt peace.

As I stood there and watched Mark, and saw Luanne standing at the kitchen window, I realized that life does go on. The children were running around under the pecan trees that have been the home to many a child and their laughter still rings in my ear. The smell of home cooked food fills the backyard and light rain is now coming down. My wife yells for me as she gathers up the boys because it's time to go. I load the boys in the Jeep and we drive past Granny Hilda's carport. Granny Hilda did not own a car, but her carport was the largest area I'd ever seen designated to sidewalk chalk for children. As the boys and I drove home, we passed the roadside country store where this story began, but it is now forever closed. Mark may think the closure of his store was a failure, but I feel he is rich with memories of running a small country store with his mother that catered to people that time has forgotten. I will remember the first time I laid eyes on Granny Hilda and no matter how old I am; I will never forget the taste of the homemade biscuits she made for me.

Jeff Mitchell & Wm. Josey Visnovske

Written in memory of Granny Hilda: your food fed us when we were hungry, your wing of love protected us when we needed protecting, your wing of fire guided us when we needed guiding and your spirit will always remind us that life goes on.

- WLV –

Anchored

We are now what we lived then. For better or worse, our memories anchor us to our past. They can guide us in our present and lead us to our future. They can be the source of our nightmares or an internal celebration that comes from those feelings of freedom we experience when we realize that we have made decisions to be different than our ancestors.

Our past does not dictate our current or future behaviors or our choices. It can only influence us. We are ultimately responsible for our choices. We can decide not to follow our parents or grandparents, but the past has a very powerful influence on most aspects of our lives and we must take the past into consideration in the present.

Josey is today a country boy brought up to appreciate the simple things of life, to cherish the goodness in people and to live time-honored traditions that could be traced back many centuries - Loyalty, Honor, Integrity, Respect, Compassion and Understanding.

Josey's stories are rich with images that evoke the smells, sounds, tastes, sights, sensations and emotions of his childhood. If we let our imaginations wander a bit, we too can find in his stories and, in our own memories, bits and pieces of our childhood. We too can remember sights and sounds and tastes that brought us joy and comfort as children. They are not only the important things of childhood. The childhood experiences have matured into the convictions that underlie adult behavior.

Most of all, we learn from Josey that the most important elements of life are the relationships we have with our families and our good friends. Human relationships, like the relationship that Josey had with Granny Hilda and Mark, are the Gorilla glue of life. They hold us together when things are rough. They, more than any riches and possessions, are the forces that make life worth living. They make the difference between adults who sneer or smile at a child with a toy yellow school bus.

- JTM -

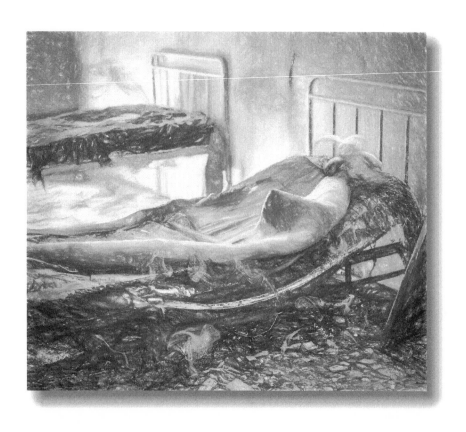

Story 6

The Last Stop

I ran down the stairs and my mom had breakfast waiting on me. As I finished the last bite of my egg sandwich, mom told me that I needed to get going or I would miss the bus. I put my homemade book bag on my shoulder and headed down the quarter mile driveway to catch the bus on the country gravel road. Our driveway was down one hill and up another hill with a creek in the middle. As I was headed up the hill, I could hear the bus coming in the distance as it rolled between the ridges. I ran the last 100 yards and was greeted by the dust from the gravel road as the bus came to a stop. Mr. Schneider opened the door and laughed as he could tell I was out of breath from running up the hill.

As the phone rang I rolled over and saw that it was 2:30 a.m. The voice was a familiar one, and he said, "I have a fire if you are available." I said, "Sure," and he said, "It's a fatality fire." As I dressed, I thought it might be possible for me to work the fire and still be home in time to make breakfast for my boys or maybe bring them breakfast. Years ago, I started a tradition that if I got called out in the middle of the night to work a fire, I would bring donuts home to my boys for breakfast. I knew of a donut shop close to where this fire was, so I thought I might be able to do my job, and also be the dad who brings his kids breakfast.

As I drove up to the fire, the smell of a burnt building was the first thing that hit me when I opened my truck door. The flashing lights from the fire trucks were bouncing off anything thing that had a reflective surface. The sound of several fire trucks idling drowned out the voices of firefighters who were standing close to where I parked. As I retrieved my camera, helmet, respirator, and put on my fire boots, the investigator who called me filled me in on the details of this fire. The husband woke up to find his house on fire. He woke up his wife and then headed for his children's room, but there was too much fire between their rooms so he exited his house, and retrieved one child from a window. The husband could not retrieve the other child and then he realized that his wife had not followed him out of the house. The father held the one child as the flames consumed the house.

I told the investigator that I would take the pictures of the inside and outside of the house if he would handle interviewing the witnesses. He said that would be fine. After I put on my helmet, respirator and fire boots, the firefighters watched me walk toward the house that was steaming from the water that was poured on the fire. The firefighters looked at me as "that guy" that comes in and figures out what caused the fire and "that guy" that puts the body in the bag. The look is one of respect and confusion as to why anyone would want to place a burnt body in a bag. As I crossed the yard, my feet felt as though my fire boots were too big, and I felt like a clown walking with big shoes. The camera took pictures of the house as my mind tried to process what the fire did inside, but in reality, my mind was in fear of what laid in the debris.

I finished the outside pictures and made my way inside the house. The roof on the right side was partially collapsed and I had to bend over to walk. The fire had consumed the floor in many places and all that was left were the wooden floor supports, so I had to balance across a two-inch board to walk. My helmet has a light on it, and for a brief moment my mind jumped back to hunting and the many times I have crossed a creek using a fallen tree. I tried to just focus on the step in front of me and not the fall if I were to lose my balance. I was able to walk standing up through the left side of the house because the floor had not been consumed by the fire. My fears were soon confirmed as I found the mother lying next to the bed. The fire damage to her body was minimal and the room still looked like a bedroom. The camera took pictures of the mother as the Rolodex file in my mind logged the pictures of the mother along with all of the other pictures I had taken from scenes like this.

I worked my way back to the right side of the house where there was much more fire damage than the left side. As I reached the middle of the house, I had to bend over again to walk, and crossing that log or, in this case, a two-inch board. Several times my helmet would hit the collapsed roof and remind me that I'm not small enough for this side of the house. The steam from the fire would fog up the lens on my camera, but I had an old washcloth to wipe the lens clear. The firefighters told us that the boy was on this side of the house and soon I found what was left of him. He had crawled under the mattress to escape the fire. There was nothing left of the mattress but the metal springs. I put one foot on one board and the other foot on the other board and squatted down. My camera kept fogging up and my breathing through my respirator sounded like Darth Vader from Star Wars. I worked my way around the mattress, taking picture after picture and tried to make sure that I did not fall through the floor or hit my head. I removed the mattress from the boy and small pieces of sheet rock that were on the mattress were now on his body. I had a small hand-held garden tool that I used to remove debris from bodies in fires. My boys have the same type of tool that they use in a place in our yard we call "the swamp". They make small creeks and ponds, and play with their toys in it. My dad had made me the same kind of place when I was a small boy. As I pulled away the debris, I finally figured out that he was lying face down. The fire damage to his body was more significant than his mother's. He appeared to be around the same age as my boys, but the fire damage was enough that

I could not tell what his race was. I continued to remove the fire debris from around his body, all the time taking picture after picture. Some of the pictures stay with the camera, but others slam into that hard-drive picture storage in my mind. I was with the boy for at least an hour and finally got all of the debris off of his body. I was ready to place him in the bag.

I walked out the front door of the house. The fire trucks were still idling and the flashing lights blinded me. I walked over to a group of firefighters and they once again gave me that look. I saw one familiar face, pulled my respirator down, and asked him if he would help me put the mother and son in the bags. He said, "Yes." The reason his face was familiar was because he had helped me put four people in bags a year ago at another fire. He is much taller than me so when we walked down to the house it looked like I was his son. I pulled my respirator down and said, "It's not pretty in there and thank you for helping me." We bagged the mother first and carried her out of the house. She was only ten feet from the back door. As we carried her, I thought, how another minute might have made a difference in her survival. She was only ten feet from the back door and how a minute sooner she might be alive. The tall firefighter and I worked our way over to the boy. I grabbed his little ankles and lifted him into the bag. I said inside my respirator, "It's going to be ok buddy, I will get you out of here." As I zipped up the bag, I could not help, but think about the times I've zipped up my boys in their sleeping bags. I made my final crossing of the boards, being careful not to drop the boy.

The sun was starting to come up as we walked back up the hill to the fire trucks. The tall firefighter looked over to me and said, "You were right it, was not pretty in there." I pulled my respirator off and could smell the burned flesh of the mother and son on my clothes. It is a smell I have learned to accept, it is a smell like no other. I stood at the back of my truck and cleaned my little garden tool and my boots that felt big on my feet. The sun was now on my face and its warmth felt good. The house below me was still steaming and the firefighters were packing up their gear. They still looked at me the same way, but they also had a look of failure. This is when it hits you, the reality of what you just did. There is no step or fall to be concerned with. The mission, the task, or whatever you call it; is done. Now, all that is left are the pictures in your mental hard drive and the vortex of emotions that swirl inside you. As I stood there trying to process this place in my life, where time has just stopped, a school bus pulls up in front of the burnt house and opens the door. I stood there frozen to the ground, unable to tell the driver that the little boy took a different bus today. After a minute, he closed the door and pulled up to the next house.

I realized then that I had missed breakfast with my boys. I called my wife, who was driving the boys to school, and told her I was sorry. I told her I felt guilty for not being there. She told me that the boys understood, but my reply to her was that I didn't understand much of anything right now. I told her I wanted to go by the school and make sure the boys were okay. She said, "Please go home, get cleaned up and do what you do." As I got off the phone, a tear shot from my eye and I knew then that this fire scene had hit home.

The drive home was like most drives home after having worked a fatality fire. I can always smell the person on my clothes. I rework the scene in my head to make sure I did not forget to do anything. Then there are the fires like this one that hit close to home and ring my bell. As the tires roll across the pavement, my mental hard drive spins in my mind, and a fatality fire that I had not thought of in years, pops back into my view.

I get home, get cleaned up, and head for the woods. My wife was right. I needed to do what I do, which is retreat to the sanctuary of the woods. I've been asked more than once why being in the woods helps to calm down that hard drive (Rolodex) in my head. I don't really have an answer. I have found that things we did as children, seem to calm the hard drive down. Maybe it's because when we were kids, most of us did not know about the harsh realities of life.

It's 3:00 am and I'm headed to a fire. I just drove by the road that leads to the house where I spent my morning with a little boy, and I still do not know his name. I have learned much since that day and I know its okay he rang my bell. I tell people that call me when they get their bell rung, that it's a reminder that we are still human. Yes, we have a job to do that some do not understand, but when we can do this job and not feel anything, it might be time to go to the house for good. I have come to realize that some fatality fires will stick with us and some will not. It does not mean we don't care about that person, it just means some hit closer to home than others. This job is like crossing a log or crossing the two-inch board, it's all about balance. We try to balance our love of family, our love of what we do, and somewhere in the middle of that balancing, we try to process the last stops that stick in our mental hard drive (Rolodex).

- WLV –

Jeff Mitchell & Wm. Josey Visnovske

Balance

"No person, no place, and no thing has any power over us, for 'we' are the only thinkers in our mind. When we create peace and harmony and balance in our minds, we will find it in our lives."

> - Louise Lynn Hay – American Author. Wrote best seller, You Can Heal Your Life in 1984 (1926-2017)

Josey inundates us in the "Last Stop" with a profusion of sensory images and actions. He runs, smells, sees and hears as a child. He then continues to add images as he works, later in his life, as a certified fire investigator. On the scene are the flashing lights from emergency equipment. There are the pungent smells of the burnt house and the burnt victims, the sounds of firefighter voices almost drowned out by the idling of the trucks. He balances himself on narrow boards, hits his helmet on parts of the house and photographs anything that might be evidence in this case. It is all part of Josey's world.

He wishes for respite from the constant drumbeat of the sights and sounds, smells and actions. Instantaneously, memories of his childhood, his family, and his hunting experiences flicker fleetingly into his mind. They do not appear because he wished for them. They are already there. Things he currently sees, hears, smells, tastes, senses and experiences in one split second in time open the door to his memory banks and what is there comes to his consciousness in a prioritized and orderly fashion. Thoughts may seem random and unimportant, but the mind is trying to provide any critical information to help with the current situation as well as reduce tension so a person can perform better. That is the mind's way of providing a 'micro-break' in the midst of a chaotic or distressing experience.

A person does not stop functioning while having a micro-break. The brain is an incredible information-processing center. It can handle thousands of memory fragments, thoughts and images in far less than a thousandth of a second. The brain doesn't just turn on when we are trying to slay a dragon. It's always on whether we are sleeping or awake — 24 / 7. Just like a fighter pilot looking at multiple data bits on his cockpit integrated helmet visor, action does not stop. The pilot interprets the information and incorporates it into his mental and physical reactions to achieve his mission.

There is no pause; there is no stop. The thoughts and memories of one's past do two things. First, they provide an information burst of potentially helpful information that warns us of potential problems and aids a person in finding a solution to a problem. In Josey's case, balancing on a narrow log as he crossed a stream in his past helped reassure him that balancing on narrow boards in a house fire required a skill set he had already developed and used earlier in his life. Second, the memories of the past can knock down the tension level a notch or two and thus refocus mental and physical energy on the task at hand. Some are surprised that memories and thoughts can calm us while performing high-intensity jobs. Calming, however, goes along with the concept that what calmed us as children will often calm us as adults.

Josey feared what he might encounter next at the scene of the fatality fire. But he had a job to do and set about completing it even though it was hard. Ultimately he handled the deceased, prepared their bodies for removal from the scene and finally put them in body bags. He even talked reassuringly to the dead little boy. He did his job with care and dignity. A key part of his job was complete.

There are some dangers associated with high risk, high intensity jobs like Josey's. Many thousands of emergency personnel face them everyday. Josey addresses at least three of the dangers in the "Last Stop." I nicknamed these three the "COG." A cog is a tooth on a gear wheel in mechanical clocks, motors, or even big machines. Cogs interact with other cogs on other gear wheels to cause machines to move and function. When I look at cogs interacting in a machine, I sometimes think that it would be painful and cause a serious injury to have one of my fingers caught in between the cogs. Then I think, figuratively, about a person being caught in a set of big cogs. The pressure can be extreme and damaging unless the machine quickly stops.

Let's look at the factors that make up the COG. Any of the three factors can generate something positive like solving a current problem based on a thought or an image that arises when the present brings up something from the past. But, many times, these three factors are associated with a negative condition or thought.

The 'C' is for Collision of Worlds. It occurs when something about one's work reminds an individual of his or her personal life. When Josey zips up the body bag, for instance, he gets an image of zipping up his children in their sleeping bags. One thought he may have had is that the little boy in the body bag could have been one of his boys. Personal connections between one's work and one's family can be disturbing and hard to shake off.

The 'O' in COG is for Old Memories. As I pointed out above, there may be some benefits associated with old memories. They can caution us to be careful or to try something to work out a problem. Old memories can also cause discomfort or pain especially if the old memory is associated with a particularly poignant loss in our lives.

The 'G' is for Guilt. Feelings of guilt are associated with thoughts that "I should have done more." Or "I could have done something different." Or "If only we had arrived a minute earlier." Guilt feelings represent thoughts that we failed and somebody suffered the consequences of our failure. (Josey feels guilty because he couldn't get home to get his kids breakfast). Our conclusion is that we have to hold ourselves responsible for whatever we think went wrong (even if we are inaccurate in our perceptions).

When the human head receives a hard blow, one common symptom is a 'ringing in the ears.' Some people describe the unpleasant experience with slang phrase like "That rang my bell." Josey uses this phrase in the story to describe the cognitive and emotional reactions he had to this particularly disturbing fatal fire.

Psychological balance, that is, the way a person thinks and the way he or she feels and behaves, can also be thrown off when someone experiences a significant traumatic event. It can make anyone feel like he or she is caught up in the negative aspects of the COG – a collision of our worlds, old disturbing memories and guilt feelings.

The brain launches into immediate and intense processes to free the person from a COG. It does everything possible to restore balance and the ability to process information. It will use memories, memory fragments, thoughts, and experiences - whatever it takes to restore cognitive and emotional balance.

- JTM –

Story 7

We Stand Witness
(A very short story)

Death, loss - being the witness is an unwelcomed comfort zone for me these days, but being a player at times and a witness at others have made me a better soul. Sometimes, I think I would rather be the player than the witness. As a witness, I allow myself to feel your pain and I so want to hold it for a bit to give you a break, but it does not work that way. I stand witness and anticipate the tears and the lack of tears, but the soul cries much harder than any tear duct could imagine. The road, the plan, the dreams seem to slide through our hands like sand. It constantly changes its form, and we witness with an overwhelming sense of helplessness. Life is not ours to plan, but to be a player and to stand witness. The moment in time that greets our face is all we have to work with. That moment in time, to me, is our purpose. We were meant to be there as a witness in that moment. It may not be the parade we thought it to be but, to whoever is facing us in their pain, our witness to them and for them, however, may be the parade of a lifetime.

- WLV -

Transition Man

Jesse Joel Smith, 1999 – 2017

Taking steps towards healing from tragedy so that we can help others.

Story 8

The Anna Smith Story

A man once told me that everyone has a story that defines them. Some of these stories are buried deep within our souls, waiting for the heavens to make sense of it all because we are beyond mankind's help. At times, these stories sit in our throats waiting for the right person to ask the why, and when the story comes out, we feel like we can once again breathe. On some days, my story is buried and other days it sticks in my throat. Today my lungs need air. Today I will tell you my story.

My name is Anna Smith. I am a Paramedic of almost 25 years. I've served in a variety of EMS services, starting in the fire service (for which I had to leave due to development of a chronic lung disease) to flight, remote and critical care medic, emergency responder to Instructor. I have served in foreign countries and domestically, through it all, I've taught others to follow the path of self-sacrifice, the path of public safety.

When I had my son Jesse, I became a mom and then a paramedic. At the tender age of eight, Jesse began to have severe headaches. I sought medical advice to decipher the chain that seemed to be locked around his head. The headaches had no pattern, no rhyme nor reason, just the pain, and what I recall to this day is the sense of helplessness. I began the desperate search for the answer that would provide my son relief. My husband and Jesse's father also battled with feelings of helplessness, a hopelessness that only grew with every rising sun.

At the age of 14, my son was diagnosed with the medical condition that bound him, and treatments soon followed. The treatments were helpful, but the pain did not end. As a proud mother, I stood by my son as he fought with courage through surgeries and pain most adults would never understand. He was my warrior. In the meantime, I learned to move between roles seamlessly. I was a paramedic, caretaker, advocate, and a wife, but as a mother my life revolved around my son. Soon it became clear that the years of caring for others before self, both personally and professionally, were taking a toll. It showed in the voids of our lives, and bled like an untreated wound.

Despite the chains around his head, Jesse tried hard to be a normal teenager. He dreamed of joining the military and becoming a pilot, but he knew a helmet would never fit over the chains wrapped around his head. He did not give up and decided to follow in his parents' footsteps. I encouraged his desire to pursue a profession in public safety but to steer clear of EMS because I know that, though rewarding, being a paramedic is like acid to the soul. Jesse, the Warrior, decided he would go into law enforcement and no chains would stop him from achieving that.

Jesse was on several medications to help control the headaches but as mentioned before, with minimal success, surgery proved to be the only definitive treatment. Subsequently, when the medications were stopped, he was hit with puberty. He was flooded with hormones and confusion as he blossomed into a man from a child overnight. I knew he was suffering through a hard transition but at the same time, I was impressed with his advancement, changes, and growth. Unfortunately, what I didn't see, was the fact that his body and mind were not handling this sudden change well, and he began suffering from depression, feeling as if he was a burden and that's when my warrior became tired. Too tired to continue.

I was Jesse's caretaker full time and his best friend; I had stepped away from the profession I loved to best care for Jesse.

He had become my whole world, my only focus. On August 25, 2017, I left Jesse to run some errands. I came home and the front door was unlocked. I yelled for Jesse and he did not answer. There were no screaming victims in this house. There were no lights and sirens, no bags of gear. Was I dreaming? What nightmare was this in my home? The poison of public safety had finally taken its toll in every cell within me and those I loved. Before me lay my son, Jesse the Warrior, who had taken bolt cutters and cut the chains around his head. His lifeless body lay on a blanket that he placed on top of the white tile floor so he would not make a mess. I stood there as mom, as a paramedic, as a screaming loved one, just like ghosts of others before, who have begged me to save their loved one. I sat next him and I could feel the untouched part of my soul being consumed by the acid of being a mom who was a paramedic to her son.

The weeks that followed were twisted and torn with the whys, what-ifs, would haves and could haves of suicide. A man once told me if you live long enough you will lose someone to suicide and cancer. I'd lost my brother to suicide; my mother to cancer but nothing devastated me more than the death of my son. Jesse fought the chains that bound his head but how could I miss the warning signs of suicide. Did the mom or the paramedic in me fail?

We were blessed to learn on the day we celebrated Jesse's short yet profound and painful life that he meant more to others than just his parents. On that dark day a ray of hope shown when hundreds came to celebrate at his memorial. Jesse somehow, between the chain links of pain, had touched others in countless ways. We placed his ashes in an urn engraved with these heartfelt words for him, and the fallen before, "If love could've saved you, you would have lived forever."

There was no relief as the emptiness consumed me; I had lost my direction, lost my purpose. I was drowning in a sea of grief, guilt, and despair. It took me over a year to realize the acid that consumed my soul did more damage than I understood. I was once again, helpless, frustrated, lost, and now bound by the very same chains that once imprisoned my son. Jesse had found the freedom he needed when he sacrificed himself for what he believed was the good of others. John 15:13 explained his truth: "Greater love has no one than this; to lay down one's life for one's friends."

Just a matter of days later, after his memorial, the heavens wept with us as Hurricane Irma, a horrific tempest, came to our unlocked front door. The mother in me found refuge in the life of a paramedic as others in need reached out, never knowing I needed them more than they needed me. I buried my pain, my grief, the reality of a life I couldn't comprehend that was my new normal

The hurricane blew past and I was once again lost. My mind was saturated with unanswered questions and a fathomless grief. Overwhelmed with suffering I became numb and after a year had passed since that fateful day, I sought help because I knew I had reached the limit of my own healing. I searched for therapy to help save my life.

My first therapist wasn't ready for the bloodstained white tile floor. The look of horror drenched her face as I unfolded my story. I had to walk away and with me came Jesse's chains, which were now wrapped around my battered lungs.
As if I was triaging my own recovery, the next stop on the road was EMDR. I had known several who had great success with it, so I tried it. I was told it does not work for everyone and as it turned out, I was the one immune to such therapy.

My next step in self-triage was a support group for parents of suicide. The monthly meetings only proved to intensify my separation from the norm and telling my story repeatedly proved more damaging then productive. It was good to not feel alone but I wanted to cut this chain from my lungs so I could breathe again.

The last stop on my triage road was another group, also suicide survivors; it proved unproductive except to show me that the chains around my lungs, the ones binding my soul were going to be there for a while. I wasn't sure I had a while. I needed relief, hope, answers, and direction. I needed to cut the chains that were suffocating me. I concluded I was on the wrong path and none of this would save me from my impending death. I had become my son.

The great architect, who goes by many names, such as coincidence or serendipity, seemed to have a plan and this time it was in the form of a former student of mine from a decade ago. We talked for hours and he listened with kindness and concern. When I told him my story he said, "I know of a guy who might be able to help you. He helped a coworker of mine. He is not a therapist and to be honest, is a little rough around the edges". It felt as if a ladder had dropped into the abyss I was in and a tiny light shown above, I could smell the sweet, fresh air of hope.

I made contact with this man. He was rough around the edges, yet kind and caring. He was an intensely private individual, but he offered his home to a stranger and said, "I doubt I will screw you up any more than you already are." My current mental healthcare providers were behind me 100%, as were my loved ones. I typed the address into my GPS and advised I would be there in seven hours. I had flown in helicopters struggling to keep a patient alive. I have traveled foreign countries fighting against another's imminent death, but today the road I was on was stained with my son's blood, his pain and haunted with memories of him. I struggled to breathe. I struggled to live but the same fight that had been in Jesse's heart, coursed like fire in my veins.

The man said he lived in the country but when the GPS took me as far as it could, I called him for guidance, but my call went to voicemail, which made my reserve flounder. My only recourse was to turn to my iron walls of self-defense and let it grow taller and stronger with every mile. Now looking thru the veil, I wondered if there was any hope at all. He too may not be able to unlock the chains around my lungs, but this fight wasn't in vain, I knew there was an answer somewhere on these country roads.

The tiny part of me that refused to give up finally found his home. To a degree he was what I expected, a country version of the Star Wars character, Yoda. Yes, that is who he was. It was time to pull off the bandage and get this over with. He seemed in no hurry to hear my story though. Even when I said, "We probably need to talk before your wife and kids come home," to him it appeared this was just another day and I was just another lost city girl who needed a place to stay for a few days. I wondered if he understood completely what he'd signed up for? I was hesitant to meet his boys, because I had a son, he was a good kid, and the idea of ill-mannered kids made me sick to my stomach.

The next few days were not what I expected even though on the phone he told me what we would be doing. I guess I thought he was joking. As hard as a tried to put my walls up around his children, I could not resist being called Ms. Anna and never grew tired of "yes ma'am." This was not their first time being exposed to a guest in their house and their dad doing what he does. They have traveled with their dad to other states and touched the hearts of those who felt they had no heart left. When his oldest asked to teach me how to weld, I said, "sure." I had no idea what welding has to do with healing but there seemed to be a method to the madness. I was fully invested regardless. Yoda's wife accepted this stranger into her home with open arms and an open heart and at that moment, over margaritas, I did not feel odd to be suicide survivor. I was a mom talking to another mom.

It became clear as the days rushed by that Yoda had a gift to heal souls or at least guide them to the path of healing. He too, like me, was stained with the blood of others but he has a gift, one powered by the pain of others to fuel his roadmap to rescue. He said more than once, "The brain likes to resolve conflict and accept a path to resolve it. The brain does not always make the best choices, so it is our job to help the brain see other pathways. Over the next few days we will introduce a few new slides to your current slide show and maybe your brain will like this path better." Basically, he had just offered to reboot my memory bank with the sweet fresh air of hope."

On one of the days, smoke covered the house and yard and he said, "They are burning the fields off today." I could see the flames in the field as the fire consumed the fallow brush. The grass returned to the earth as ashes and landed in my hands. I breathed in the rich, smoky air and let it fill my damaged lungs. It was the earths' rebirth; it was pure. Though still hard to breath, it was relief.

We toured the land around his home and I took the seat of a student. I listened to the stories, hearing more than just words, yet Yoda's method was still unclear to me. I figured I would just go with the flow. Yoda introduced me to a friend of the family, a retired farmer named John. He showed me his farm that he farmed with his father. It was a simple life without airports, bleeding patients, and bloodstained tile but not without its own conflict. John was a man just happy to see the next sunrise.

Transition Man

Yoda's boys gave me a tour of their farm and in the distance I could hear gunfire. As the lump in my throat grew, I knew the time had come. I had developed an intense phobia to firearms and no matter what, I now knew and accepted the reality that Jesse would have found a way to cut the chains from around his head, even though he had chosen a firearm to do it. As we pulled up to the small concrete pad with a roof, Yoda sat there in camouflage, behind a rifle as though he was born there. His children took their place as if rehearsed, but in a natural, organic way. We watched his finger ease the trigger back and the shot rang out. I felt my heart beat rise and my brows furrow in confusion, but I knew I was in a safe place. I could smell the gunpowder and the fear of this moment was not the fear I thought it to be. I was in a cocoon spun of trees and green grass, with people who were but strangers, who days before had opened their hearts and souls to a suicide survivor. Yes, I am a survivor.

Camouflaged Yoda walked the distance to the target with his youngest son, and returned with a smirk on his face and a new slide for my life's slide show. The moment was frozen like a photograph, with a cold, calculating clearness of thought, the edges painfully sharp as my hands folded around the warm steel. My heart slowed and as my breath eased, I now felt hope. Yoda spoke calmly and compassionately as I placed my finger on the trigger and eased it back. The shot rang out and with it came a loud boom. I laughed aloud because the boom was a surprise. The method to his madness had become a little clearer. Those who've seen the video of this moment saw the chains break and watched the broken woman take a step closer to healing—a step closer to life.

Our tour of the farm continued to a pond with a modest cabin with no electricity or running water. I could tell this was close to the core of Yoda, where he went to escape the brutalities of this world. We had now entered his sacred ground. His children shot pistols as I sat and watched. The lump in my throat eased and the air to my lungs seem to be less but as the pond waters echoed the gunfire, a salve of healing grew from his children. Children trained and educated on safe practices of firearms; children who hunt to feed their family; children who do not have a chain around their head; children who broke the walls of a mom who is a paramedic. I placed the pistol in my hand and with Yoda by my side he once again became the teacher and I the student. I eased the trigger back and the water erupted before me. The ripples found their way to pond bank and stopped. In that moment, the air flowed into my bound lungs and when the next round hit the water, I could now taste the healing cool forest air as it flowed freely into my lungs. Yoda was no longer by my side but he was with me, I just could not see him, as I knew Jesse was too. I shot until the lump in my throat was gone and the smell of gunpowder was no longer in the air. I heard the words as the shot rang out: "I am a survivor of suicide,"

The last stop on our tour of the farm was like a very country version of a Disney ride. We were in a utility vehicle being driven by one of his boys. We crossed a creek with mud flying and we landed in the swamp. Yoda led the way with his children next to me as my forestry bodyguards, trying to keep me out of the mud. He told me to buy rubber boots before coming but I thought he was joking. As I avoided the mud, the creek next to us spoke to me as I can only assume it speaks to this family. Yoda told me of their adventures here in what was clearly his place to wash away the blood of death and scars of life. I cannot say I felt complete here but I understood completely why they did, and what it meant when a family of strangers opened their home to a woman battered and broken by life. As the utility vehicle carried us through the mud on our way out of the swamp these words echoed in my head: "He has cast me into the mire, and I have become like dust and ashes," Job 30:19.

My last evening was spent with a home cooked meal around a warm fire pit behind Yoda's house. He cooked a meal over an open flame and farmer John and his wife came to join us under the star filled sky and peace found its way to us as the flames crackled. My mind still rambled over all the new experiences and memories and even though the company was good, I could still see the bloodstained white tile floors, but for once, it did not paralyze me in the moment. I could still breathe.

The next day my departure time was changed due to my work so I informed Yoda I was leaving sooner than planned. He had been building a desk for a friend while I was there and was putting a coat of varnish on it when he did what he called his "exit interview." The compassionate teacher knelt before me and with every brush stroke he painted a masterpiece. He told me a story I am confident no one had heard before and I could see his emotions bursting out. He warned me what he was about to say might sting a little and he said, "This ain't a paying job so this is just the way I see it". He was correct—his words did sting, but they were true. True words from a man on his knees with a paint brush in his hands and his heart lying on that concrete floor before me; he is now a friend who was once a stranger. As if he went to the shelf and grabbed a bolt cutter, my chains fell to that concrete floor and laid down next to his heart—the heart of an odd man I'd met just a few days ago. His final words to me were, "You have a story to tell so go and spread the word."

With a cooler of frozen meat his family harvested from the earth and a Tupperware full of chicken that was cooked over an open flame, I set my GPS for home. On my keychain, a memento with a bullet hole and sharp edges to remind me of all the moments, all the slides I had to add to my life's slide show, played again and again on my drive home as I showed my brain another way to resolve the conflict.

The ladder that dropped in my abyss when Yoda came to be, gave me insight, and when I could see, I accepted. Once accepted, I became accountable. Once accountable, I had to make a choice. I had to find the courage to conquer my fears and weaknesses and continue or fall back and regroup. I'm not the type to surrender, so I chose my path and learned to resolve and overcome conflict. I knew I was no longer walking alone.

I like answers; I suppose we all do. I like to understand, to learn, to grow, and I tend to analyze things. The method to his madness—I had no answer to it, no science to define it, but like magic I was in a place of healing. I have grown to understand much of life will go without answers or explanation and it will vary from the greatest moments of joy to the truly horrific. I know somewhere between the burning fields, the gunfire, the muck of the swamp, the ripple of the pond, a family of strangers, and Yoda in camouflage (who really was rough around the edges), I now had hope and direction.

Since that trip down the triage highway, the intensity of simplicity has had time to absorb. The lessons learned, the healing made, the growth achieved, and the relationships developed are now entwined in the very fibers of me, associating the good as the swamp creek water washing the disassociate memories clean, because there will always be pain cutting off my air, and like the heavy load this life is, I am strong enough to carry it. I stand in the mire with ashes in the air but I can breathe. My son, my Jesse is in the air we breathe, still touching souls from wherever he is, and I am no fool and know there will be days that are hard and even though the chains are not gone, I have found the strength within to carry them.

Transition Man

I am starting to recognize myself again, as the person my son was so proud of. I am slowly but surely waking up and stronger than ever. Without guidance, support, encouragement and the dedication and love of others, I would be another statistic, but today I stand before you as a work in progress, walking hand in hand with hope and direction as my best of friends.

There is a way out of this. There is always hope.

My name is Anna Smith, my family lost our son Jesse Smith to suicide, and yes, we are survivors!

Jeff Mitchell & Wm. Josey Visnovske

Yoda and the Wounded Soul

With the permission of Anna, Josey wrote the Anna Smith story in the first person. He wrote it from Anna's perspective. Josey asked Anna to write about her son's suicide and her time at Josey's home. His objective was to further ingrain the new "slides" into her processing the tragedy of her terrible loss. Anna sent Josey 12 pages of emotions jammed into those pages. Josey read those pages before bed one night and at 4 a.m. his head began to spin through those pages and the days he spent with her. Since Josey does most of his processing by writing, he knew he had to write. Six hours later, the Anna Smith story was finished. He had written it as if he was Anna. Josey felt that he had to become her in his written words to process the 12 pages and his time with her. He said it was one of the hardest things he has ever written.

Josey forwarded it to Anna to see what she thought. She made a few changes. She decided to call him "Yoda." Josey is known for the nicknames he gives people and now he has one.

This is the first time in any of our books that we have written about suicide. Suicide is the ripple in the pond that Josey spoke of in the story. The bullet may pierce the water but the ripple continues on and on. Suicide is the one of the most difficult traumas to work though. It can never be forgotten. It lingers, like a life sentence, in the minds and hearts of every one who loved the person who chose a permanent solution to life's temporary pain and problems. Suicide wounds the soul.

Our aim in this story is to demonstrate that a wounded soul can heal from the trauma of suicide. The profound loss suffered by the family and friends of a person who completed suicide, however, is not healed by one intervention alone. Instead, there is a complex interrelationship of many factors that

93

prepares the wounded soul for recovery. In Anna's case, several forms of psychotherapy may have prepared her for her visit to Josey and his family. A new environment, fresh air, the right timing and some new activities like shooting a firearm while at Josey's home may have helped her to see her life in a whole new way. Certainly care, respect, and a listening ear contributed to Anna's coming to terms with the suicide of her son. There are many things that can help a person like Anna climb the stairs blocked by the trauma of suicide.

— JTM —

Jeff Mitchell & Wm. Josey Visnovske

Story 9

Amazing Grace

Dan and I stood in the fencerow of cedar trees trying to get some shade from the summer sun. In the distance I could hear Mr. Bill's tractor running along the long rock road that led to his hillside farm. In front of us was a field of corn that Mr. Bill planted some months ago and a group of hungry crows were doing their best to eat his corn crop. Mr. Bill pulled up on his old Ford tractor that had made a living for him and his wife for many years. We never knew why Mr. Bill did not have kids, but he treated us kids that lived on the county gravel road like we were his own. Mr. Bill pushed in the clutch with his left foot, moved the gearshift to neutral and shut the tractor off. As he stepped off the tractor with his blue jean bib overalls, old straw hat, worn leather boots, and a small tobacco stain in the corner of his mouth, he smiled at us. The smile was followed by, "Boys the crows done gotten in my corn patch and I need you to stop them." We told Mr. Bill we would take care of the crows but we would need to set us up a summer camp in the cedar thicket behind us. He smiled and said "Sure." I think we thought we pulled a fast one on Mr. Bill, but he probably knew we always wanted to have a reason to build a campfire and helping farmers always gave us access to more land to roam and hunt. A few days later, I found myself sitting with my family in the Catholic Church that all of us folks who lived on that country gravel road attended. My best friend Dan's family was not sitting far from us. Mr. Bill, besides being one of our local farmers, also played the organ at our church. He sat in the choir all by himself. Sometimes when he would mess up, his wife Mrs. Hilda would yell up to him and tell him what verse to play. It was hard not to laugh, but sometimes we smiled instead.

Transition Man

My mom crawled up in my Jeep with what she called her new knee made from recycled plastic and beer cans. My two boys crawled in the back of the Jeep and we headed down a two lane black top road. My mom's 77 years of gray hair blew in the wind. It's hot today and the air conditioning worked in my Jeep, but a large part of me thought that the Lord did not intend for us to live all of our time in air conditioning. I explained to my mom that a local farmer called me about hogs getting into the 1000 acres of sweet corn he had planted. The farmer wanted my help.

My oldest son is 12 and the first time I killed a wild hog was when he was inside my wife. I was deer hunting along the swamp and at first I thought it was a bear, but soon realized it was a hog. I shot the hog and called my pregnant wife to help me drag it out so we could eat it. That is a story inside a story as they say. I had no idea how much damage a hog could do to crops until the farmer next to our farm called and said, "Hogs are coming out of your swamp and have eaten 40 acres of my corn." I taught myself to trap them with large traps and snares. I would hunt them during the day and eventually I started hunting them at night. Everything I knew about trapping and hunting hogs was from all the mistakes I had made; which sometimes feels like life.

As we drove down the two lane black top road, my mom commented on the lay of the land since this is my home and not hers, she lives some 700 miles from here. In the distance I could see the top of the large irrigation system that gives the corn what it needs most, water. The irrigation system has a pivot point in the center of the field and when it's running it slowly pivots around the field giving the corn the closest thing to a God-given rain shower. At the edge of field sat a pickup truck and I told my mom that is the farmer who called me. The truck is new and fancy and my two boys seem to know more about it than me. We pulled up to the fancy truck and the farmer stepped out in shorts, a t-shirt, and tennis shoes. He introduced himself to my mom and said it would be easier for us to go in his truck to look at where the hogs are entering the field. My mom said she would rather just sit in the Jeep and wait. Mom grew up on a hillside farm and I guess sitting next to a sweet corn field and being able to watch a herd of cattle across the road was a much better site than looking for hogs.

The boys and I piled in the farmers truck and I thought that the cool air conditioning felt good to the boys. We circled the field and the farmer parked next to a patch of woods. The farmer said, "There is a cypress pond down in there and the hogs come from there and enter the field here." I said, "Ok, we will take a look and see what kind of hog sign we can find down in there." As if it were a fire drill my boys got out of the truck and headed towards the woods without being told. The farmer said, "Where they going?" I said, "To look for hog trails and hog sign." As the boys neared the woods they split apart and all I could see was the dust that surrounded their Wranglers and cowboy boots. I smiled at the farmer and said, "I better get going."

The boys and I found several well used hog trails and down near the cypress pond big places where the hogs had rolled in the pond mud. It's an amazing thing to watch your children blossom and turn into men. I remember those times with my dad and thinking he was the strongest man on earth as he picked up a big chunks of wood we used for firewood. It was not until years later that dad's true strength shown through as he died in the house he built. I know in his eyes he appeared weak, but true strength had very little to do with how physically strong he was, it's how strong his soul was.

The cypress pond was beautiful, it was a hidden treasure to my eyes, but the hogs had done their best to make it ugly. The boys and I busted out to the woods and found the farmer next to his truck. I explained we could set snares and I could bring one of my big traps up, but I would need to also hunt them at night. The farmer said, "I have 10 fields of sweet corn which is around a 1000 acres but as of now this is the only field they are in." I said, "The hog sign around that pond tells me these hogs have been here for a long time, so they are not going anywhere unless we help them go somewhere." I could see the fear in his eyes with all he had invested in this 1000-acre crop and he was up against a beast that operates mostly in the darkness. I told him I have an expensive rifle that has a thermal scope so I can see the heat from any animal at night. I explained to him that hogs have a greater sense of smell than most animals, so I have to hunt them with the wind in my face so they cannot smell me. I could see a sense of relief in the words that came from my mouth, but his fear was still there. I told him I had to go out of town for a week, but when I returned my boys and I would do our best to save this crop from the hogs. We drove back to mom who was just as content as when we left her. Mom always seems to just be glad she is alive even if she has a knee made from recycled plastic and beer cans.

For the next week I was surrounded by asphalt, concrete, trees planted by man, people, and everywhere I went was air conditioning, I thought hard about that sweet corn field and how I wished I was there instead of in that city. Good people surrounded me and I appreciate that, but I was tired and I needed my space. I needed to hear myself think and wanted all my senses alive. When I'm in the concrete jungle it's as if some of my senses start to shut down. The ground under my feet is always flat, the air is always cool; there are no birds to hear. Every thing I see was made by man.

I was at a conference where people like me gather to discuss and learn about how traumatic events affect us. The learning is good, but for many, the discussions take them to dark places where they recall their own trauma or traumatic stories that's been told to them. I can recall most of the traumatic stories that have been told to me. I can see people's faces as their souls twist and turn as they try and make sense of this beast that thrives inside them. They cry out in fear of the uncontrolled emotions and feelings that run through their head. Most of them fear the darkness of night. That is when God intended for us to sleep. As my father used to say, "The Lord set the sun so we could rest and brought her back up so we could work." The darkness becomes the enemy and they pray for the light of day. Some pray that you siting there will tell them what they are feeling or thinking is normal and they are not losing their minds. Some pray for peace inside them and that the beast will die. Some feel their prayers will never be answered and the light of day will never come and sadly some take their own life.

As I drove the 13 hours home from the concrete jungle I could see the sweet corn field in my mind. I could smell the fresh earth and that certain smell the corn makes as the ears of corn start to form. The hogs also know that smell and they will travel to find the source of that smell. I learned years ago that my reentry into my family's life is less like a Hallmark card and more like a turbulent asteroid with fire. They are glad to see me, but they have adapted to me being gone and when I fly in it disrupts the dad-being-gone system they operate under. My dog seems to be more in line with a Hallmark card. He will give me a series of kisses and then he will lay his body against mine as if I am holding him up but I'm sure he is holding me up.

A few days after the asteroid fire has dwindled, my boys and I make the ride up to the sweet corn field. Behind my Jeep is a trailer with one of our big hog traps on it. The day is hot and it's just after lunch. I pick out a spot to assemble the trap in the edge of the woods. My boys carry what they can to me and we put the trap together. I watch them as they watch me be a strong daddy. They try so hard to be strong and I tell them their day will come, but for now just do what you can. I grab my snare backpack and make my way along the edge of the pond showing my boys how to set snares. After a few lessons learned I let them practice and stumble and fall. My oldest sticks to me like glue but the youngest one likes to wander. I remind him that hogs are just like people, they are going to fight you or run from you so don't wander too far.

We all walk back out into the edge of the field and in front of us is the sweet corn and for a moment I thought I could see Mr. Bill and my best friend Dan. I told my boys I was about your age when Dan and I started putting up square hay bales. If the counter on the hay baler said 250 then we were paid 5 cents a bale, but you might handle that same bale 3 times from the field to the barn. I told them it was some of the hardest work I had ever done and I would not change it for anything. I told them about Mr. Bill and another farmer named Mr. Leroy and how those men never had a tractor with air conditioning. As we rode home my youngest stuck his hand out the window and did that plane thing with his hand. Something even to this day, I do it.

We just tucked the boys in bed and I kissed my wife and said I won't be gone long. She said, "Please be careful." I said, "I will." I could tell by the look on her face and after 21 years of marriage she does not "get" my need to go out into the dark of night and chase hogs. Our six freezers are full of meat so why do I have to go hunt hogs in the middle of the night when I just got home from being gone for over a week. She knows the answer but does not "get" why going to the woods or in the dark helps me get back to basics; get back to me. She does not "get it' but she supports it and I guess that's what matters.

I stop on the two lane black top road and see which way the wind is blowing. I park my Jeep and put on my vest that has extra pouches for rifle magazines and handgun magazines. I grab my rifle that looks like some high tech video camera is strapped to the top of it. I put on my old worn camouflage 'boonie' hat that has a United States Marine Corps Eagle Globe and Anchor pin attached to it. Also strapped to the side of the boonie hat is a small rubber alligator. That is another story inside a story. The wind is in my face and I sneak along the edge of the sweet corn field. It's dark, but if I use a flashlight it might spook the hogs. My feet can feel the uneven soil and in the distance I can hear the large pump feeding water to the irrigation system. Even though its night, it's still hot and the first drops of sweat roll down my back. My eyes are of little use to me. I can see the difference in the darkness of the sweet corn and the open field, but it's more of my feet telling me where I'm going.

I recall the day we drove around the field with the farmer and try to remember that to help guide me to the place near the cypress pond. I stop every 50 yards and raise my rifle and turn on my thermal scope. I scan the area between the sweet corn and woods, but no hogs. The brief details inside the scope tell me I'm not lost. I continue on until I reach a fencerow that separates two of the sweet corn fields. The fence now guides me to a spot I had picked out days ago where I will wait for the hogs to enter the field. I once again look through my scope and I'm at the right spot near the cypress pond. I see no hogs in the scope, only darkness. I get inside the fencerow and sit down next to the tree. Like my hand out the window of the Jeep, I have sat next to a tree in a fencerow since I was a child. I can hear the irrigation system in the field behind me now. The pivot has moved and it sounds like rain hitting the sweet corn.

It's now midnight and I'm where I need to be. I have dreamed about being right here since the day I met the farmer. Since the day my mom sat contently in the Jeep many miles from her home just glad to be alive even with a knee made from recycled plastic and beer cans. Since the days I lived in the concrete jungle surrounded by good-hearted people who carry the darkness with them even on sunny days. Since that hot afternoon when my boys and I stood here and heard stories of how it used to be.

I raised my rifle and looked through the scope and there he is. The beast. He came from the cypress pond and was in a part of the field before it turned into sweet corn. Before I could make my shot, he moved into the sweet corn. The sweet corn is too dense and the thermal scope will not see into the corn. I'm now blind again. I wait for his return, but he does not come back into the open spot. I think of my youngest, the wanderer, and I wander over there. The soil under my shoes tells me the hogs have been tearing the field up looking for food. I occasionally lift my rifle and look through the scope, but no hogs. I can tell I am closer to the sweet corn because it's darker to my eyes. Then a sound I know well rings in my ears, it's the bark of a hog that is startled. At this close range my rifle will be of no use. I shoulder my rifle and pull my pistol from my vest and wait. I can hear multiple hogs running through the sweet corn to the right. I hear an occasional grunt, but nothing tells me whether these hogs want to fight or flee. I stand as still as I can and let my ears do their job. I hear nothing, but I feel something. It's not my sense of touch, but it's my sixth sense or gut telling me turn around. I turn around slowly, but I cannot see anything. I cannot hear anything. I feel my heart pounding. My brain is on full alert and begging my five senses for something to tell me to fight or flee. I holster my handgun and raise my rifle and right in front of me is the beast. I shot him and five more in a matter of seconds.

My nose sucks in the gunpowder and recalls all the times before it has sucked in gunpowder. As my heart rate comes down, I laugh and smile as I recall a speaker at the conference who said a study was done and only 16 percent of the time was our sixth sense right. Maybe they did not study people like me.

I piled the hogs up and took a picture with my phone and sent it to the farmer. I texted, "It's a start". I walked back to the Jeep and even got a shower from the irrigation system and that felt so good. I drove down to the pile of hogs and loaded them on the trailer behind my Jeep. I turned my lights off and sat there in the dark. The darkness for me brings back the calm waters of our little fishing cabin, as Dad and I would check the catfish limb lines late at night. The darkness for me brings back the hills Dan and I would climb following a no count worthless raccoon hound that would only bark at trees with mice in them. The darkness never scares me; it calms me. The darkness makes me feel alive.

I get home and load the hogs into my walk in cooler where after some rest I will process the hogs and smoke the meat. My smoked hog meat has been enjoyed from coast to coast and many men and women have broken bread with my hog meat in front of them. To see a broken heart, a broken soul, or someone in need of the light of day smile and laugh while eating something that farmers live in fear of tells me the wild hog does have a purpose here. I crawl into bed at 4:30 am and my wife says, "Did you do any good?" I said, "We got some hogs and I think the asteroid fire is just about out." After a few hours sleep, I process the hogs and the meat hits the smoker. As my family comes home from school and work, sitting on table are smoked ribs. My boys dive in like they have not eaten in months. My oldest says, "Best ribs ever daddy".

Some time later, my wife and I are sitting in church with our oldest son between us. It's a special mass for his class only. I look around the church to see whom I recognize and then do what I always do. I tell my brain its not twenty years ago and it does not matter if someone recognizes me and tells everyone I'm a police officer. For over six years, when I lived undercover, I always scanned the crowds of any place I went to make sure I did not run into someone who really knew who I was. No matter how hard I try my poor brain is still trying to keep me alive and in a fight or flight mode. It might be twenty years ago, but to my brain it was twenty seconds ago. I cannot say I'm a church going man. I go a few times a year and my mind is always in some field or in the woods while I'm here. My boys always say daddy's church is in the woods.

I look up near the ceiling and through the stained glass I can see a tree limb weaving back and forth. The wind is blowing hard and then comes the rain. The rain is so hard it is difficult to hear what the priest is saying. As the rain comes down, I can see it rolling off the sweet corn stalks one drip at a time. I can see the creek on our farm beginning to fill up and water wrapping around roots that learned years ago this was a good place to grow. I can see the magnolia leaves when they land a certain way and fill up with water like a small boat. As the rain comes down, now I can feel it. I feel it run down the side of my face. My son bumped my elbow and then it dawned on me I was in church and the rain on my face was tears.

I wiped the tears from my face and the story in my head that I had been writing since the asteroid fire came home with me now wanted to be completed. I had called the story the 'Darkness.' Most of the story was done in my head, but I did not have an ending. I've been questioned by many how and when do I write and for most of my life it's when I'm in the woods, but today it's in this church. I did my best to shove that urge to write in my head into a sub waiting room, but it would have no part of that.

In the distance a child's faint voice could be heard and despite the rain and wind I could hear her and only her. I stood on my tiptoes but could not see the microphone she was singing into. To me the words were not clear, but her voice was that of pure innocence. As if a keyboard was in my head, the words could not be typed fast enough. I struggled to be that strong man, but the tears were coming. A break in the storm came and I heard these words, "Was blind, but now I see." I grabbed the hymnal from my son who looked at me like I was crazy and the song was Amazing Grace. I hit the backspace button I my head and changed the title to this story. I read the words to Amazing Grace and after 48 years of living and many childhood Catholic school masses, I finally "got" the words to Amazing Grace.

To me a traumatized person is just like the farmer trying to combat and conquer a beast that thrives in the darkness. The more I learn about the human brain and the more I understand how its sole purpose is to keep us alive, the more I understand why we react the way we do. I have a friend who is a physical therapist and she has taught me much about the human body and how it too, like the mind, is always trying to help us adapt, compensate, and overcome. She has become a part of my system to maintain balance in my body. Her knowledge of the body and why the body does what is does to adapt to an injury calms my fears that I may not do what I once could do. I call my friend Magic Joy because she heals me so I can help heal others.

Once I was able to explain to the farmer how a hog operates, it calmed his fears. Once he knew his battle was not alone, it supported him. The picture of the dead hogs in the early morning hours gave him the sunrise without the sun. The more

107

we can explain to a traumatized person the ins and outs of our brain and why most things boil down to fight or flight, it's like looking through a thermal scope, you can see the beast.

I was blessed at birth with a connection to the earth and most of what I have learned is more from watching others stumble and fall, but some of my greatest lessons came from when I fell myself. As I call it, my system, which is multiple things I need to do to balance and process my life and the lives of others that have touched mine. As I said, I was blessed because I figured this out years ago that we all need a system. This was before I even knew the brain had more layers than husks on an ear of corn. We just sat down and the priest is talking again. The rain has stopped and I'm pretty sure no one saw the rain on the side of my face. I'd give anything to hear Mrs. Hilda yell at Mr. Bill up in the choir loft right now, but that will not happen.

Mr. Bill lived to be 95. Mr. Bill never had a tractor with air conditioning and the only irrigation system he had was a thing called prayer. Years after his death, I saw one of those little funeral cards on Dan's work bench in his basement. As I type these words to you, I have two stuck to a filing cabinet from my dad and my friend Lee. I guess that's what you do with those things.

It's been weeks since I left the concrete jungle and I finally feel like myself again. This will be story number two since I got back. I've done three hog smokes since I got back and many people have enjoyed an animal that few understand and fear. I've gone for more runs through the woods than normal, but that's all part of my system. My family has finally put out the asteroid fire and the turbulence is gone. My dog is leaning on me less and I'm loving on him more. As for Amazing Grace you might wonder what I saw that day in the church. I don't think I saw it; I felt it. Our part in life, if you ask me, is to help others see not just in the darkness but in the light of day. Our part in life is to help others who are lost inside themselves find their way back home. Our part in life is to help others conquer their fears even if their fears are inside them. Our part in life is to help others want to feel and embrace the senses that were given to us to keep us going until we are 95.

I just walked into the edge of the sweet corn field and it's dark, very dark, but God is it amazing!

Amazing grace! How sweet the sound
That saved a wretch like me!
I once was lost, but now am found;
Was blind, but now I see.

'Twas grace that taught my heart to fear,
And grace my fears relieved;
How precious did that grace appear
The hour I first believed.

Through many dangers, toils and snares,
I have already come;
'Tis grace hath brought me safe thus far,
And grace will lead me home.

The Lord has promised good to me,
His Word my hope secures;
He will my Shield and Portion be,
As long as life endures.

Yea, when this flesh and heart shall fail,
And mortal life shall cease,
I shall possess, within the veil,
A life of joy and peace.

The earth shall soon dissolve like snow,
The sun forbear to shine;
But God, who called me here below,

Will be forever mine.

When we've been there ten thousand years,
Bright shining as the sun,
We've no less days to sing God's praise
Than when we'd first begun.

- John Newton, published 1779: verse 7; anonymous,
published 1829

- WLV –

Jeff Mitchell & Wm. Josey Visnovske

The Attic

Like a visit to a marvelous attic, Josey's present brings him back to the past and his past eventually leads him back to his present. He invites us along for the tour. As he does in many of his stories, he begins telling a tale from his childhood. Then he links one experience to another and then another and so on until there is a string of literary pearls from which we, his readers, can draw inspiration for our lives.

Lucky for him and for us as well, Josey's childhood was a happy one in the presence of stable and caring parents and good friends to support him and guide him in his growth. He can go to his attic whenever he needs to find something to guide him in his present situations and circumstances. He uses the wisdom he has stored in his attic over the years to touch the lives of others, either in person or through his stories.

He is willing to share his attic with people who don't have a happy attic to go to. Their attics are dark, gloomy and scary. They are filled with horrible childhood experiences that cause distress and depression whenever they venture into them. Mostly, people with dark attics avoid them. They hurt now because they lack the pearls of the past that can comfort them and guide them in the present.

If you know the man, Josey, like I do, then you will know that he is a guardian and a caretaker of those in physical pain or emotional need. He is always ready to protect and help others who are struggling with any number of concerns or issues. He doesn't put a price tag of his willingness to aid others. He reaches out and makes a difference for others because it satisfies some internal and inexplicable drive within him to lighten the load for anyone he perceives to need a boost. In a sense, he views other care as self care. Satisfying the drive to assist others soothes that internal guardian trait of vigilance, the need to watch over those who may be vulnerable. He subscribes to the philosophy of the great Winston Churchill who said, "We make a living by what we get, but we make a life by what we give."

On this tour of Josey's attic he presents some interesting contrasts between darkness and light, feelings of being trapped, closed in, and agitated as opposed to being free and at ease. He does this by his description of a country guy in a concrete jungle, as he describes cities. A city visit for him is dark and depressing. He appreciates the good people he met at the conference and the information and training he has received, but the steel, concrete, glass and the trees that seem out of place make him restless for the fields, woodlands and swamps of his home.

There are some important pearls of wisdom, Josey, brought out of his attic. They include the art of returning home, a recovery system, adjustment and being careful not to deaden the senses.

Returning to home from a visit to the concrete jungle, or anywhere away from home, for that matter, requires a careful approach for those who were left behind. It is not as simple as turning the key and walking in the door. They have grown accustomed to life without you even if only for a few days. You have temporarily lost you place in the wolf pack and you can't expect the people you love to simply turn off all their adjustments to life without you in a second's time.

Let them know when you are returning. Also let them know if you are running late so they know to continue their adjustments and routines for a while longer. Don't expect parades, balloons, surprise parties and the like when you get home. Other than the initial welcome home, those who stayed behind are still on the 'you are away' mode and might treat you a bit like you are not there. Kids are particularly good at not noticing you are around. Don't be offended. They will catch on in time. Sometimes they have to work through some resentment feelings. Remember, they were left behind. It doesn't matter that you left for work. They were still left behind. Don't approach your teens with a heavy-handed attitude. Lighten up a little. You will be able to resume your place in the pack in a reasonable time but you can't push it too hard. Keep in mind that little things that went wrong at home while you were away are big to the people who had to handle those things even if they are no big deal to you. Patience, stay calm and carry on!

Being away has it own problems. Coming back home has another set of problems. You need some adjustment time just as your family needs it. You have to recover from whatever negative things you encountered while away. There are almost always some negatives. Establish a routine. Find a place where you can process the away experience. That place will be different for just about anybody. It is a matter of personal preference. Do your routine in an orderly manner.

You need to work out a system of recovery that helps you to care for your body and mind. Get Exercise, food, rest, relaxation, sleep, meditation, prayer, and have contact with friends and family. Let your family know when you need some alone time. Reinsert yourself into your family life by gently taking on your usual responsibilities but without unnecessary pressure or fanfare. Resistant family members will gradually accept you back into your normal role within the family.

Josey's system includes going to the woods in all kinds of weather, staying awake and alert for many hours for days at a time while he hunts for wild hogs. That might not work for everyone. I suggest, therefore, that each person develop his or her own system for recovery.

Josey believes that recovery can be achieved faster and more efficiently if a person does not deaden their senses in any way.

Instead, keeping the senses sharp and at peak performance helps to focus one's attention on something positive. Had Josey not paid close attention to all of his senses while he was hunting, he could have been seriously hurt or even killed by a wild hog.

Among the most important things that people need in their self-care system is openness to inspiration. Being inspired by something or someone means that our spirits are uplifted and excited. Inspiration gives us new ideas; we can make better plans and we can carry out those plans with renewed enthusiasm. Inspiration makes us feel more fulfilled and valued as a person. Inspired people face challenges directly and with courage and perseverance.

By the name of Josey's story, 'Amazing Grace,' one can justifiably conclude that he was inspired while in church. Not all inspirations come from church. Some come our teachers, firefighters, police officers, emergency medical personnel, doctors and nurses, civic leaders, our military personnel as well as our spouses, children, family and even strangers we meet. Sometimes you have to look in your own attic and you can inspire yourself.

"Inspiration is hard to come by. You have to take it where you find it."

-Bob Dylan, American songwriter and singer –

– JTM –

Jeff Mitchell & Wm. Josey Visnovske

Story 10

The Interview

We drove down the one lane gravel road. In the distance I could see the barn and the house behind it. My dad told us, as the rocks popped under the tires, that he worked with the man that lived in this house and if we bought the farm across the road from him, we would be his neighbors. As we pulled up in front of the house, the man and his wife greeted us. Dad told us he had children and, from behind a tree in the yard, I saw a boy taller than me. His blond hair stood out, as he stood there looking at what was now in his yard. Like a herd of cattle, we followed the man into the house. The parents sat at the kitchen table and us kids found our way into a room at the back of the house. The room had a sofa and television. We sat there trying to find a common thread from the life we had 25 miles from here, but the threads never came, at least not then. Our fathers worked together, but it would be many years before the threads came together and made some memories.

I walked up the long steps to the second floor of the sheriff's office and entered the room. I had met the sheriff a few times, but did not really know him. I had my two-year degree in my hand, but he never asked about it. The man who I would really be working for was in the room, but said very little. The sheriff asked a few questions I was not sure how to answer, but the man smiled as if my answer was perfect. I was nervous and rubbed my hands until I found a splinter from the cedar tree that I had used to build a fence post the day before on a neighbor's farm. As the sheriff spoke, my mind drifted back to the hill and how I was still not done building that fence. I could see the green grass and could always hear a vehicle coming long before I could see it, as it drove down the gravel road that separated many farms in this place we called home.

The sheriff said, "I think you will work out just fine." As the sheriff stood up I managed to dig the splinter from my hand and as we shook hands the splinter found its way to the floor.

I stood there in the detached garage with my long hair and beard as she held me tight. She told me, "They will be fine with you." I said, "Look at me, who would want their daughter dating a man like me?" She said, "It's not who you are, its just the way you have to look to do the job you do, they will understand." I said, "I cannot really talk about my work." She said, "Its ok I'm the one in love with you, not them." She backed up and smiled at me and even though it was dark I could see the girl who took my heart many years ago. She said, "Let me go talk to them and then we will go in together." I watched her enter the back of the house and then my mind drifted back to a time when my face was clean, my hair short, and I was younger. I remembered the first time I walked in this house some 10 years ago. I was nervous and scared as I met her parents. I knew they knew me as the boy who rode the Harley to school, but not as the boy who truly loved their daughter. The love I had for their daughter scared me more than anything I had seen in 16 years of living. I stood there in the detached garage, peering through the window as she spoke to them in the kitchen. Through the window I could see they had not changed much in ten years, but I had. I still rode a Harley; I still loved their daughter. I was still scared of that love, and under this mask I had seen things I wished I could forget. I left her ten years ago and returned ten years later because the love was still there. I still did not understand the word love, but I understood the word comfort. I understood, even in a detached dark garage, the distant sense of her made me complete and calmed the uncertainty of life.

She walked out of the house and entered the garage. She said, "They are ready for you." The sidewalk to the house was narrow and she walked in front of me and held my hand.

Before we entered the house I asked, "Do they know I'm a police officer?" She said, "Yes, and they know not to ask any questions about where you work and not to tell anyone about you." I said, "I'm sorry it has to be like this." She smiled and squeezed my hand and said, "I love you."

I stood there in front of the fancy hotel bathroom mirror and wiped the tears from my eyes. The necklace my wife bought for me, after she cashed in the six years of change I had collected when I lived undercover, was outside my t-shirt. The Saint Michael medal hangs from that necklace and I rub it between my thumb and finger before I tuck it under my t-shirt. In my shirt pocket I can feel the collection of dog tags, coins, and medals that tell me some of my memories are real and this is not dream. I can see the gray in my hair and my eyes look tired. An hour ago I was on a stage in front of 300 people telling them a sad story about a man I met a year ago. I seem to know a lot of sad stories these days, but many have a glimmer of hope at the end. The man stood with me or I stood with him, as we told our story to that group. I did my best to fight the tears, but they came as my mask fell to the floor.

I walked out of the fancy bathroom and saw the man and woman waiting for me. The man was younger than me and did not dress like me. He had on purple socks that made me think of the lilacs that grow wild many miles from this place and how I wished I were there and not here. The man was a reporter who wanted to hear my story and why a small town was so dear to my heart. The woman worked for the same people I did, and it was her job was to make sure I did not say anything out of line. I had met her a few hours before, and she heard me speak to the group, so there was no point in using a mask. She had seen the tears and felt the pain. Her outfit and shoes looked very uncomfortable, but she fit in more with the reporter than I did.

Transition Man

My old camouflage backpack sat on the ground near me and in this fancy hotel in the middle of an asphalt and concrete jungle, that backpack told me I was alone. I heard them speak and they did their best to comfort me, but the tears were already there so I waited for the interview questions. The woman, who I had just named Dorothy in my head, sat there like a coiled rattlesnake waiting to stop me from saying something I would regret. I leaned forward to hear the soft-spoken reporter and felt my belt buckle against my stomach. I then thought of my friend the G-Man who was dead and this too was not a dream, but wearing his belt buckle was very real. I said a few words before the tape was turned on, but, to be honest, I cannot recall one of the words as they are forever lost in that asphalt, concrete jungle.

I saw the reporter press the button and I thought about the hundreds of times I recorded my drug transactions as I lived undercover. I thought and felt the fear that I would get caught recording someone and even though that was 20 years ago it seems like yesterday. I could not help but feel the reporter was swinging an ax and I was the tree. It was like he was looking for an answer, but did not know what he was looking for until several layers of my bark had been removed and the red cedar was exposed. Careful and delicate are the best words to describe the reporter with the first swing on the ax. The reporter had just returned from a small town where a sad story was told to him that happened over four years ago. The reporter heard of a man who kept returning to the small town and I was that man.

The reporter continued to swing his ax and with each blow the memories came out. I knew the story was sad because I had been there after "it" had happened. However, the people I met were no longer just people. They had become my friends. The reporter wanted to know, when I first met them, had I used any special training to gain their trust. I reached into my shirt

120

pocket and handed him the collection of dog tags, coins, and medals. Many have held them when they speak of their sad day; not a man wearing purple socks, but this man was about to hear about four years of very sad days. I told him how I shot a quarter for my father and he added a few medals and then others added things as the sad stories collected around a ring. Most of my heroes have died and their dog tags found their way to that ring. Dorothy had relaxed and was no longer sitting like a coiled rattlesnake, but her face told me she was hearing the sad story. The reporter was no longer in his asphalt, concrete jungle, but he was with me as I told him the story of that small town. He had been there; he knew the dead, the injured, and the ones who just wanted to be left alone. Though that small town was many miles away, we walked down the streets, through the cemeteries, and where "it" happened.

I fought the tears, but the battle was lost. Things that happened over the four years that were not sad at the time, now caused the tears to come more rapidly. I would look at Dorothy from time to time with embarrassment, but the mask was long gone. To be honest, I did not care. The tears were a part of the story more than the words from my mouth. The reporter swung the ax less, but the red cedar still poured from me. At times I could tell the reporter felt bad for opening up these wounds. Was this what he was searching for? Was I answering his questions? I looked past him and outside this concrete tomb was a tree planted by man and manicured to be appealing to the eye. The green leaves spoke to me and, for a brief moment, I was where I needed to be, not here telling a sad story about a small town. I was in my woods "with trees God had planted" and, there, nothing is manicured.

The reporter asked less and less questions and I just told the story. I told him about the first time I went to that small town because it was my job, but every time since then it was my part of this thing we call life. I realized then, the story about this small town was being told from the inside looking out and how was that possible since I'm not from there. I was not there when "it" happened. I lost no one there that I knew. So why do I feel like I'm telling a story about a long chapter in my life? Why do I feel the pain and loss of those who survived? Why am I crying as I tell this story? Why am I holding my ring of medals so tightly?

I look at Dorothy and the reporter, and realize this is not what they thought it would be. To be honest, it's not what I thought it would be. As the four years spun in my head and people with other sad stories seem to enter back into my head, I attempted to complete the story of that small town. The reluctant, delicate reporter asked about the small plastic rabbits that I have given to those who have shared their sad stories with me. I reach into my worn camouflage backpack and retrieve a rabbit. I handed it to the reporter who holds it in his hand as I have seen many people do. The reporter is different now. He has felt and seen the pain. A few weeks ago he walked the streets that four years ago were filled with panic and fear. He walked the green grass at the cemeteries and saw where people, doing their part, have found a place to rest and there one can feel peace.

A few weeks ago, I saw him walk into the station the night after the fourth memorial service. We glared at this outsider entering our sanctuary without permission. I saw the Mother Hen, who happens to be my recovering, emotionally wounded friend, approach him and within minutes she smiled. I approached him and he said he would like to speak with me, but I simply said, "Only if my work will allow it."

The reporter looked up with rabbit in hand and said, "What should this story be about?" I showed him a picture I had taken hours before he stepped into the station that night. He said, "Where was that taken?" I said, "Where "it" happened". I told him we go there every anniversary date and walk the flat ground where "it" happened, but this year they smiled so I took a picture." I said, "They accepted "it." Now they have accepted the outcome and that is your story."

The reporter placed the rabbit on the table next to the recorder. I stood up and shook the reporter's hand and commented on his purple socks and handed him the rabbit. Though he did not tell me his sad story, he heard and felt mine and maybe the rabbit will remind him to do his part, not just his job. We stood there as complete strangers, but between us was a small town that time had forgotten. I said, "I think I got more out of that town than they got out of me." He walked away and soon he was just another person in the asphalt, concrete jungle, but he took a piece of me with him.

The reporter left and Dorothy and I sat and talked. I felt bad for her since this was not a factual interview, but an emotionally charged interview with a man she had just met. I could tell she wanted to comfort me but she did not know what to say or do. Sometimes comfort is not saying anything, it's just the way you look at someone.

I drove for 13 hours and at 4 a.m. my head and heart hit the pillow. The subtle smell of my love's shampoo comforts me as I feel once again as if I'm in a detached dark garage. The interview, the story, the asphalt and concrete jungle, and the highway between there and here spin in my head. In her sleepy state, she reaches over and rubs my leg and says, "I'm glad you are home." I lay there for two hours as the end of the highway finally caught up with me and then I found myself in the kitchen, to see two young men I had not seen in over a week. The youngest was ten today and the oldest will be twelve tomorrow. I recall how the nurses had handed me these young boys and once again I was not sure what questions they would ask me, so I told them a story as I held them in my arms.

It's been a week since that interview and I am where I belong, in my trees that God has planted. I'm on my unmarked trail through the woods, as I run in search of comfort and trying to find a place for these things called unexpected emotions. In an asphalt and concrete jungle, inside a concrete tomb, a man wearing purple socks asked a question about a small town where something very sad had happened. Three hours later he still did not get his answer, but I did. The interview showed me that I am on the inside of this small town and even though I was not there when "it" happened I allowed myself to feel their pain, so I could help them heal. As the rabbit sat alone on the table, so did those people in that small town after "it" happened. They did not ask for someone to come back, but I did because I know what it feels like to be alone and I had to do my part, not just my job. I realize now, from a man with purple socks, that we have healed together, because we were in pain together. I realize now, just like the people in that small town, I too wanted to know someone cared even if it was from a man wearing purple socks.

As the trees passed by me, my feet ground me back to this earth, and to me, life is a series of constant interviews. When we hug each other, when we shake the worn hand of a man who has a story behind his eyes, when we hold a new baby, when we tell a sad or happy story to a group of strangers, when we fail to answers the questions; but just tell a story, when we sit quietly and just observe, and when we place our hand on the shoulder of someone who feels alone, these are the interviews of life. We all want to feel accepted, loved, and remembered. We all want to know someone cares even if he is a stranger and wears purple socks.

-WLV-

Anxiety

Every person has some anxiety. Some people have fairly low levels of anxiety; others are more anxious. With the low-level anxiety, folks appear calm and unruffled when circumstances grow tense. Even the toughest of the tough and the roughest of the rough, however, have their anxious moments. People who claim to have no anxiety whatsoever are either ignorant of the functions of the brain and its interaction with the physical body or they are flat out lying. In either case they typically end up dead long before their expiration date.

Anxiety is part of our evolutionary make up. Its purpose is to help us to recognize threats in our environment and to steer clear of them. We naturally move away from situations that cause a spike in our anxiety levels. We are naturally fearful of dark places, large spiders, snakes, weird creatures, and strange people with weapons. Enough anxiety will generate fear. Anxiety and fear can be a driving force that enables us to fight for our survival or run away if that is more likely to help us survive. A moderate level of anxiety helps us to think fast and act fast. Anxiety can be our best friend. It can save our lives.

Some people have excessive amounts of anxiety, which can interfere with daily life. It can cause, among many things, a decrease in clear thinking, withdrawal from contact with others, memory problems, and it can cause people to freeze up and become unable to take actions in their own best interests. Excessive anxiety can disrupt our problem solving and decision-making processes and our concentration. It can cause us to make minor and major mistakes. Excessive anxiety can produce a number of physical and emotional reactions including muscle tremors, shaking of hands and fingers, headaches, difficulties in breathing, immobilizing fear and panic attacks. Too much of it can make us mentally and physically dysfunctional.

There are innumerable things that can make people anxious. A bad report card, criticism by a spouse or a boss, an auto accident, conflict in the workplace, testimony in a court, loss of a credit card, a big repair bill and just about anything that makes us concerned or worried. Josey was anxious at 16 when he was falling in love. After ten years of not seeing the girl he loved so much he returns to her and he experiences anxiety when he has to meet her parents again.

Having to make a public presentation or to engage in a media interview when someone is a pretty private person can also make people anxious. If a person has spent six years working undercover and living amongst criminals, public contact can be the source of anxiety. That describes Josey's circumstances exactly. He is not overwhelmed or out of control, but he doesn't care for the public's view into his life. The pending interview is viewed as a threat.

Josey's mind instantly kicks into defense and control mode. His mind goes to old childhood memories and then to memories of his police officer days and then to the love of his life. The brain does that for two reasons. One is to help calm the system so he can continue to think his way through the current anxiety. Second, the brain goes to old stuff to see if there is anything back in the brain's storage banks that will help him to deal with the current perceived threat.

Next Josey scans through his memories of the subject of the interview – the town where a very sad thing happened. The scanning of the memories of the town is sort of a review of his mental notes so that he will be prepared to answer questions in the interview.

The brain is all about recognition of threat or potential treat, calming the physical system, review of pertinent memories that might help now, and alerting all battle stations to prepare to engage the threat. All of these mind functions take place in a microsecond or two. In an instant, in a heartbeat, one is changed and alert and ready to deal with whatever a person is facing.

Being alert and ready does not mean a person is happy and excited about what is coming. Threats of the unexpected remain. The "What ifs" are running through our minds non stop and will continue to do so as long as we stay on alert and feel threatened. A high state of alert is maintained for the duration. You don't have to like what is happening to you. You just have to get through it.

It is always helpful and reassuring if someone checks on your welfare when you are facing difficult or challenging times. It won't take away the threat, but it is encouraging to us that someone took the time to ask us if we are okay. We should never assume that others in the midst of challenging times are doing just fine. It is always better if we actually check on them. The reporter and the representative of Josey's work place ask him several times if he is okay or if he needs a break.

Josey spent a lot of time and expended a lot of emotional energy toward the people in the town where some people died when a sad thing happened there. He visited several times over several years to stand as a witness to the townspeople's suffering. He had great compassion for them.

Compassion is an expression of empathy for people who are suffering misfortune. It is uplifting and inspiring to people in psychological pain. But it is not free. People who are genuinely compassionate toward others may feel some emotional pain themselves.

There are some professions that are particularly vulnerable to a condition called compassion fatigue. Doctors, nurses, therapists, mental health professionals, dentists, and people who work with disaster and trauma victims may feel some of the emotional pain. Some people feel it so intensely that they have to stop working with those in emotional distress. They develop compassion fatigue. They begin to believe that they no longer have anything left to give to others. They can either get therapy to deal with the compassion fatigue or they will continue to grow more and more unhappy with their work with people. When that happens, they often begin to find other professions to engage in. They know that they cannot continue on in a profession that demands a great deal of compassion from them. They know they cannot fake compassion. The people they would like to help are not dumb; they are just distressed. People in distress can sense fake compassion as soon as they encounter it. They will reject help from anyone who tries to fool them into believing that the helper really cares. Or, if they don't reject it, they will certainly resent it.

The tears Josey describes come from absorbing some of the pain the people he cares about have expressed. It is okay to feel the pain of others as long as you have a system built up to help you recover. Josey has such a system.

> "There are moments when all anxiety and stated toil are becalmed in the infinite leisure and repose of nature." - Henry David Thoreau (1817-1862), American Essayist, Poet, Philosopher.

– JTM –

Jeff Mitchell & Wm. Josey Visnovske

Story 11

The Jacket

Dad stood there in the garage, leaning against his homemade workbench, telling me that the rock quarry and the union did not agree on the new work contract. Dad said he and the other guys were going to strike. I sat there on the steps that lead into the house with my feet on the concrete floor and never felt so ungrounded to the earth. Even though it was May, and the early summer south breeze was coming through the rear garage door, it felt cold.

I was graduating from high school in a few weeks and not going off to college. I already worked full time at a grocery store that was 25 miles from our home. Dad said, "I'm not sure how this will all turn out and we might need your help." My dad was a man of few words, but he spoke that day and so did the look of rejection on his face.

The next year was one I think my family has tried to forget. My dad had to swallow his pride and do whatever to make ends meet. Mom, who for the most part was a stay home mom most of my childhood, also did whatever to make ends meet. My mom's dad was special, but not the kind of special that comes to mind for most folks. Dad did not speak to him for reasons most of us have tried to forget, but we took money from him to keep from losing our home. Dad never called in sick and always worked when asked, but after 22 years of dedication none of that mattered. A year later, a broken, rejected man returned to the quarry to make less money than he did ten years prior. Dad was never the same after that year of rejection. In theory, my life, as an adult, had just begun, but that year taught all of us something. Dad carried that year with him, but in a place that he tried to hide. He hid it well, but at

131

times his stride was shorter, his smile was less, and his face was different.

I could see a small light in the corner of the room. At first, I thought I was in a hotel room, but the cover on my bed felt like a hand sewn quilt. I then woke up enough to realize that I was in Ben's room. Ben was the son of my wife's Aunt Kathy. He was killed in Iraq back in 2003. I wrote a story about him many years ago and this past spring my doctor friend and I put Ben's story in book two, Sister Mary, the Baker, the Barber and the Bricklayer. I mailed a copy of the book to Aunt Kathy who I did not really know, but I thought she would enjoy seeing a story about her son in a book. Aunt Kathy reached out to me afterward and over the last six months, an Aunt who I did not know very well became a part of my life and my family's life. My boys were right down the hallway sleeping in another room and my wife was back home. I got up, made Ben's bed, and was amazed at the beautiful quilt made from his military patches. I stood and looked at the small, lighted case that displayed Ben's military career. On top of the case sat a small plastic rabbit that no one in this house had asked where it came from or why.

I walked down the hallway, woke up my oldest son, and asked, "You want to hunt?" He rubbed his eyes and said, "Yes." I woke up my youngest son and asked, "You want to hunt?" He said, "I think I will sleep in." I said, "Ok." I told him, "I will be back before we leave for church and Aunt Kathy and Uncle Bill are right down the hallway if you need something." I asked my oldest son, "Do you want to hunt with me or Cousin Danny?" He said, "I want to hunt with Cousin Danny." Cousin Danny drove up shortly thereafter and I watched them drive down into the bottom below Aunt Kathy's house.

I recalled Uncle Bill's directions to drive past the hog house and follow the edge of the field. When you get to a big tree in a smaller field, past a gate, park there. I parked my truck and as I got out the cold northern wind cut through me. I put my backpack on and grabbed my rifle. Once again, following Uncle Bill's directions, I walked down into a bottom, crossed a small creek, and came to a small patch of woods with the foundation to an old home. The sun was not up yet, but I could see enough that I did not need my flashlight. Uncle Bill said, "You will see a round thing with tin on it, that's the deer stand that overlooks the bottom below." In the faint, dark distance a round odd object appeared. I lowered my head, entered it, and found a chair, a few empty soda bottles, and the wrappers from hand warmers. Our thousand-mile drive, not much sleep, two young boys cooped up in the cab of a truck has brought me here. It never ceases to amaze me what people can make a deer-stand out of. My best guess, in the dark light, was at some point this round object was used to contain large electric wire, but I would think from a plane above it looked like a UFO.

Uncle Bill called it the Rack Off Place. I have learned after years of hunting that every place, and every spot, has a special name, and if it is not obvious as to why it is called what it is called, just accept it, like I accepted Algebra, and I never understood any of that.

As the sun peaked its way into my day, the frost-covered ground told me it was cold, but my fingers and toes also told me it was cold. Many years ago, I had helped a friend on his family farm. I noticed that the temperature had dropped and I had driven my Harley. Wearing no gloves and old cowboy boots, I started up the Harley and rode the 25 miles' home to my parent's house. Mom heard my Harley enter the garage and came out to find my hands stuck to the handlebars. That was 33 years ago, but the damage to my fingers and toes is permanent. I break out the hand and toe warmers, and begin the process to bring them back to life with the rest of my body.

I recall and reflect on a statement dad always said, 'Son, somebody has it worse." I look down at the bottom below and even though it's much colder than what I am used to, this is my church. My boys say it often when I head off to the woods, "Daddy is going to church to clear his head." I look at my watch and think of my wife who is still in bed sleeping on her left side. After 22 years of marriage, she is not really just my wife anymore. In my head, I refer to her as the other part of me. When we are apart there is hole in me, a sense of incompleteness. The thought of there not being another part of me scares me more than death itself. The sun is now up and the frost-covered ground is as grateful as I am for the big ball in the sky that lights our way and warms our day.

I see movement in the bottom below and he steps out like the king of his domain. His horns signify this is his world and I am a stranger sitting in a UFO. As he walks, I can see his muscles moving and flexing. Aunt Kathy told me I could shoot a doe or a buck, but today my time here is not about shooting. The buck below is in his moment, like I have been many times, and then the rug gets pulled out from under you and you are left there broken. Though the meat would be a blessing to Aunt Kathy and her family, the memory I need now is not one of broken, but where the buck goes on to have his day, and I too go on to have my day. The buck blessed me with a few more minutes of him in his moment and then he continued down through the frost-covered bottom. He stopped and looked back at the UFO where I could see the warm air break from nostrils. In a frost-covered bottom, two creatures of God shared a moment and a memory. As the buck disappeared into the woods, the thing that keeps us humans moving forward told me, it was time for me to leave my church, and join the church that mankind has created.

I make my way back to Aunt Kathy's house to find my youngest son ready to go. My oldest son said, "We saw some does but none were close enough to shoot." We change clothes and drive down the gravel road to the small Catholic Church, which is Aunt Kathy's second home. As we enter the church, like the statue of a saint, Aunt Kathy is sitting there in her spot. I am reluctant to sit that close to her. My life has been less than perfect. To some, in this small church, I am a stranger, but over the last six months, they have seen the man and two boys who sit next to Aunt Kathy.

As I wait for mass to begin, I stick my hands in my coat pockets and grab the hand warmers from my morning hunt to warm my hands back up. I hear a sound unlike the footsteps coming into church, it's a wheel chair, and it's similar to the one my father used after cancer found its way to him. Cousin Danny's daughter drives the wheelchair. She was born with muscular dystrophy 14 years ago. The sight of her, and knowing her story, is the definition of a miracle that she is still with us. She can only move one finger on her body. My cold hands tell me my father's words, "Son, somebody has it worse." Aunt Kathy smiles at the sight of her granddaughter because she knows the struggle and fight the child has done to just breathe.

As the priest begins the mass, my mind wonders to every tree, every valley, and every creek that I have sought peace from in the world that lays out here. In my pocket are a collection of religious medals, dog tags, and things from people I have met in what I call the manmade tornadoes of life. A few months ago, on a visit here, Aunt Kathy gave me one of Ben's dog tags. I run it between my fingers as if it has magic or maybe it will bring me peace. Ben is buried behind the church with a modest gravestone that marks the spot where he left this world in his moment. He died doing what he loved. As I rotate the objects in my hand, I think of those of you that are still with me, and realize our relationships were joined when you were broken. Somehow those relationships are much stronger than any other ones I have. Before I know it mass is over and I think I heard one word, Amen.

We have breakfast at Aunt Kathy's other daughter's house. She lives on the family farm. I am a stranger here, but they treat me like I'm not. The house is filled with extended family, big and small. I can hear the sounds of young kids playing as their laughter floods every part of my brain. Aunt Kathy and Uncle Bill sit with me, but it's Aunt Kathy who can see right through me. It has become apparent that Aunt Kathy and I have connected in a way that I do not understand, but have accepted. As we eat our breakfast, Aunt Kathy fills her tube up with her special milk and feeds her stomach direct. A constant reminder the cancer is back and there is no treatment. My father's words ring in my ears, "Son, somebody has it worse."

We stood in the family room and held hands as Aunt Kathy said a prayer for our safe travels. Aunt Kathy hugged me and we had a moment. I stood there and held her bones wrapped in years of flesh and faith. In the corner of the room a constant candle burns for Ben, but Aunt Kathy feels blessed that she still has five other children. It became clear to me on our first visit to this holy land some months ago that a simple story of Aunt Kathy's life would not do her justice nor to those of you that would read about her. I asked her permission to write a book about her life. She asked, "Why?" I said, "You have something we all search for. You have faith in life." She said, "You mean faith in God?" I said, "No ma'am, faith in life."

With that and like a scene from the old television show, the Walton's, we drove away down the gravel road with Aunt Kathy, Uncle Bill, and their son Sam standing on the front porch. My boys asked the same question they always ask when we leave, "Will we ever see Aunt Kathy again?' This time I answered differently. I said, "Boys, we could all punch out at any time. You could have six months with Aunt Kathy or never have known her. That's life. You cannot love and not hurt, or you can love and make memories, the choice is yours." The two young boys did not hesitate in their response, "We will take the six months' daddy."

As we made the three-hour drive to my parent's home, the heaviness of the holy land faded in the distance with the help of country songs from the classics. As they call it now, classic country music, it takes me back to the garage I grew up in. My dad always had this old radio near the back door with an extra wire wrapped around the antenna to pick up a station that was too far from our home. When he was done working in the garage, he always unplugged the radio and that told me he was done with what he was doing. As we drove, I recalled a recent trip where we left Aunt Kathy's house and Merle Haggard sang a song about how we as a society are 'a snowball headed for hell.'

I remembered that song being played in our garage when it was not a classic and it was just country music. If I study then and I study now, seems like Merle may be right. In the truck, sit the future of the country, two young snowballs trying to grow up and be snowmen. I do my best to teach them the ways of the Lord, how to be a man, and the basics my dad taught me, but many days I feel I fail them. Three hours passed and the familiar sound of gravel pops under the truck tires, which tells me, we are close to my parent's home. As I drive down the ¼-mile driveway, it seems to be longer this time than last time. Even though I walked it as a boy, twice a day, to catch the school bus, this driveway gets longer with my age. I guess I know the reality of what lies at the end of the driveway now, it is more than just a childhood home where I was that snowball. As we crest the hill, I can see the house lights through the tall pines. My truck lights shine on a concrete statue that marks the spot where I buried my childhood dog. In the seconds as I pass that spot I relive years of her life and the moments, to include the moments that still pain me to this day. No one is home at the moment, but we unload and I get the boys ready for bed. I ask the same old question, "Anybody hunting in the morning?" The boys answer softly, "I think we want to sleep in."

I wake before my alarm goes off and wonder how the other part of me is doing. I walked through the field behind the house as the sun makes its way into our day. I climb a deer stand that sits next to the old pond and watch the field next to the barn. Once again, my fingers and toes remind me of that day, and once again, I can hear my father's words. The sun shows me the fruit trees my dad planted by the barn and then the reality sinks in. Next to the barn marks the spot where dad is now. A concrete eagle on top of a brick column with a small part that contains his ashes marks his spot. I think it's ironic that dad is surrounded by concrete and its products. The rock quarry that broke him was actually a plant that made concrete.

I spent the morning in the field talking to dad, I guess. I looked for deer. At times they could have been right in front of me, but I was really not there. I talked to dad about the snowballs that were sleeping in the house he built. I asked him if I was doing it right and was he proud of the man I was trying so hard to be? The hours slipped by and the sun overhead told me it was time to give up my perch and check on my snowballs. I walked by the place that marks the spot where dad had his moment that most of us try to forget, those decaying years it took for him to get there.

I have my backpack on with my water, thermos of hot green tea, trail mix and extra hand and toe warmers. I carry what I need to make it through a day of hunting. Dad carried the rejection from the quarry until he took his last breath. Mom must have seen me crossing the field behind the house and hugged me at the back door of the garage. Mom's hugs have changed in the six years since dad left us. She is still my mom, but she is the other part of dad that asked him to let go and begged him to give up and go on. I would have done the same thing, but I am sure mom carries dad's last breath with her every day.

The boys and I prepared for our evening hunt by cutting tree limbs and laying them on top of two round hay bales that faced the field next to the barn. I put an old lawn chair between the hay bales for my oldest son to sit on and I knew he could figure out the rest. My youngest son and I went down into the woods to a spot where we built a deer stand a year or so ago. The stand was six feet by six feet with a roof and was elevated. We built stairs up to it so mom could maybe sit there and reflect on things. I made a wooden sign inside that reads, "In memory of the Old Boar," my dad's nickname.

We sat there as the sun decided to leave us for the day and I told my youngest son that when I was a kid I would watch that tree right there for squirrels to come out of. I looked down the hill and saw the spot that I sat at many years ago after Christmas morning. Mom and dad somehow found the money to buy me an old used 20-gauge shotgun for Christmas. As soon as Christmas morning was over I found myself sitting next to a tree watching that squirrel tree so I could break in my new shotgun. I was around 12 years old and that afternoon will forever stay etched in my mind. I sat there and felt a sense of belonging with the woods around me. I felt peace. I felt I was home. My life was good, but that feeling was one I had never felt before and from that point forward the woods became my home. Even when I sit with family and friends, my heart is here, in the woods. The trees, the fresh earth, and the sense of belonging are what I never feel when I am surrounded by what mankind has made.

My youngest son brings me back to the here and now and says, "Daddy, a deer." The rifle cracks and mankind has spoken, the deer runs up the hill and falls over. Unlike the television shows, we hug and I fight the tears of joy. I say, "Congratulations, you have just done something that has not been done in 39 years. Grandpa killed two deer in his life and the last one was killed right over there 39 years ago. When I was growing up I always hunted on the farms we worked on, so you are the first one with our last name to kill a deer on the farm in 39 years." My youngest son's smile was even bigger now. As we walked, up to the doe, a shot rang out and mankind spoke again. Mankind spoke a third time with a text from my oldest son saying he shot a doe in the field by the barn.

As we all walked back to the house, the lights guided two generations of hunters. My mom heard the shots and waited by the back garage door. She hugged both boys and told them about the 39 years before this day, when the other part of her killed a deer on that hillside by the creek. We gathered the deer and mom took a picture with the boys. The moon was bright enough where I could see the concrete that holds my dad in the field. I hope he is proud of his snowballs. I got a rope from the garage to hoist the deer up in the wood shed so I could clean them and saw that old radio siting on dad's workbench. The electric cord was stiff but I plugged the radio in and it played. I dialed a classic country station in and by the moon light and man's light, we took two of God's creatures and transformed them into memories and food.

The boys said they were sleeping in so I was hunting solo this morning. As I made my breakfast, I thought for a moment about the old black and white television we had in the kitchen when I was a child. It was long gone. On the table sat a flat-screen color television. The days of antennae are gone and now it's a dish pointing to the stars above. I searched for something to watch and to my surprise; the old black and white Lone Ranger show was on. The same one I watched as a child before I would walk the quarter mile to catch the school bus. I took this as a sign that today was the day that I needed to break out the special rifle and I knew exactly where I would hunt this morning. I pulled my dad's deer rifle from the case and walked down the driveway. There was no doubt I had an extra stride in my step with the stars aligning above to make this a hunt I would always remember.

I walked down the hill and climbed up in a deer stand watching the same deer trail my dad did 39 years ago. Deer do not live 39 years, but like our behavior, it is learned and followed. I was cold, but the goose bumps I felt were not from the cold, but the intense sense of belonging, and the hope that I could do something my dad did. The trail crossed the driveway and from my perch, I could see part of the driveway. I spent the morning going up and down that driveway in my head. Sometimes I was a kid, sometimes I was a confused teenager, sometimes I was a husband, a father, and sometimes I was just lost.

Dad's rifle sat there with me and it was a constant reminder that it's now my rifle. The goose bumps left and the sun overhead told me maybe next year. I could see his subtle smile and hear dad's words, "That's life, does not always work out like you hope." As we loaded the truck for our trip home, the boys hugged my mom. The drive down the driveway was long. We crossed the deer trail and I looked to my right and said good-bye to the spot in the woods that has become the key to my balance. We all need a system to balance the unpredictable nature of life.

To most, my boys and I have logged way too many miles on the highways of America. Due to us living away from family and when I can take them on a work trips, we have found comfort in the cab of many different vehicles. If you ask me, some of the best quality time I have had with my boys is on our road trips or being in the woods. The terrain changes and soon we are back home. The boys hug the other part of me and the stories are now being told of great hunts, cold weather, and yes, those 39 years. The magic man runs to me, I kneel down, and wet kisses consume my face. I'm not sure he knows he has magic, but he does. Dogs have always had magic in my book. Somehow, they can just make things better by being a dog; humans have never mastered that skill.

At 4:17 a.m. my phone rings and it's one of the local guys I work with. He says, "I know you just got home, but I have a fire if you are available." I said, "Sure, text me the address." I drive two hours and pull up in front of a burnt out house. The flashing lights and the toxic smell of burnt plastics thicken the air around the house. I see my local guy and his face is one of comfort as we have been through a lot over the years. Most of the time our job is full of laughter and kidding as we do what we do, but this morning the laughter is gone. The reality of what is in the house is soon to be real as we climb the steps up the front porch. The roof is caving in, the walls are falling down, and the floor is full of holes and beginning to fail. It's hard to describe the next several hours as we took three body bags out of the house. It's hard to describe the family that is left behind, as they stand there in total disbelief. They stand there looking at us for answers as to the how and why, but this time we have no answers. My local guy and I do our best to comfort the family and even at one point, we fought the tears. The moment of that morning is one I carry with me, but that moment, as horrible as it was, is something that has further bonded my local guy and me. On that morning, we were stripped of our titles, our ages, the organizations we worked for, and, most of all, our egos. We were two men who were not only doing a job, but also doing what was right to get some people to a better place. Even though I was not physically hurt, I was a victim of a manmade tornado.

The next few weeks passed at a faster speed than I would prefer and the reality that our five-month deer season was coming to an end soon. My time in the woods is to gather food for the year to come, process my thoughts, heal my soul, and write to you. The last few years have been a challenge for me. Dad always said, "Do it right or don't do it at all." I follow my heart, I follow my sixth sense, and sometimes that does not align with those around me. I sit here today some 20 feet off the ground and reflect on the last few years. On a wall in our house is a quote from Ralph Waldo Emerson. It has been there since I can remember and to be honest I'm not sure why it has that honor, but it's there. I know it by heart and I say the words on days like today.

> "To laugh often and much; to win the respect of intelligent people and affection of children; to learn the appreciation of honest critics and endure the betrayal of false friends; to appreciate beauty; to find the best in others; to leave the world a little bit better, whether by a healthy child, a garden patch, or a redeemed social condition; to know even one life has breathed easier because you have lived. This is to have succeeded."

The last few years I have seen others more concerned with the mark they make in life versus how they made the mark. I have recently felt the betrayal of false friends and that is coming from a guy who does not have a lot of friends. Like the child who burned his hand with a hot cup of tea, he is cautious with every teacup that comes his way. The scar on his hand is a constant reminder that life is full of rejections, failures, and pain. After all, we are human. The woods are not only a sense of belonging to me, but also a place of peace. It's safe here. I am safe here.

The phone rang and it was a familiar voice. My friend said, "I guess you heard the news?" I said, "What news?" My friend said, "They found him and he is no longer missing, it's now a homicide." Those words sunk in deep and a case I had assisted with many years ago just came crashing down on me. I never expected that phone call and never expected that it would hit that hard. I never met the missing guy, he was a stranger, but I knew his life like it was my own. As my friend continued to talk, the flow of emotions flooded my soul, and that beach ball that I kept shoving down all those years came up with a powerful force. I hung up the phone and cried. It's hard to explain why I cried for a man I never met. Maybe because I felt bad that the system failed him and I'm a part of that system. I cannot be everywhere and God knows we cannot control people's actions, but this case had been in my backpack for many years; my backpack of things that needed to be completed. My boys saw the tears and they knew of the case, but not the man. The other part of me did her best to comfort me and now I stood in the yard, the victim of another man-made tornado. I looked behind the house and I could see the woods calling me.

The next morning, some 20 feet off the ground, I watched the sun bless me with her presence. Not only did she warm my body, but somehow she reached inside my soul and did her best to heal it. I spent the day trying to figure out why his body being found was hitting me so hard. In my heart, I always knew he was not missing. I cried for him more than once and as darkness fell upon my perch, it was time to return to mankind. When I walked into the house, the other part of me and the 'snowballs' were home. I guess my face and my stride told a story that did not need explaining. Before I could say a word, my phone rang and it was the missing guy's mother, we had not spoken in years.

She asked how I was and I said, "Not good." I told her, "The pain I feel is deep and it hurts more than when mom called me to tell me dad had died." I sat in the rocking chair that's in our bedroom and we talked for two hours. Last time I recall sitting in that chair was when mom called to tell me dad was dead. That was six years ago. She said, "I used to tell myself that my late husband was talking to you and guiding you when you worked the case, but now I know it was my son. Do you agree?" I said, "Somebody was guiding me." Over the course of the two hours we cried, we laughed, and I guess we mourned. She said, "You never met my son, but if God made a duplicate of my son it would have been you." I said, "I'm sorry the system failed you and your family." Meaning, I felt bad that I couldn't do more. She said, "Don't you feel bad, you did your part, you all did your part."

The next week I cried every day for a man I never met. The trees I hid in could not hide me from the pain that I felt. My system to process was on over load. I did my best to shut mankind out, but the walls of my system failed like they do in a house fire. The classic country songs spun through my head, but a song from the days after high school came to land on a limb next to me. The band was called R.E.M and they were not country and never played on my dad's garage radio. The song was called "Everybody Hurts." The song never made sense to me until this day, this tree, this moment in time. Then one morning, like in the movie Forest Gump, I stopped crying like Forest Gump stopped running. The pain was less and at least now I could feel something else.

I spent the day with the creek below, winding through the swamp, and the trees seemed to stand motionless against the wind that chilled the air around me. Darkness landed on my perch, but the moon guided me home. I walked in the house and sat down on the sofa. The other part of me said, "What's wrong?" I said, "Why do you ask?" She said, "Because you are sitting down on the sofa." I said, "I know the clinical definition of depression. I have spoken to depressed people. I know the signs and symptoms of depression. I'm pretty sure I've been depressed." The other part of me is a woman of few words. She said, "Why are you depressed?" My hand and heart were on the release valve to what I call the "container of life," that is the container inside of me that seems to be an abyss that collects the emotions that don't have a home. The emotions stay there in the abyss and spin around until they have to come out. Her gentle nudge was enough to bump my hand and open the valve. I said, "I told Aunt Kathy the other day that I'm losing my patience for people. Why can't people be stand up and loyal? Why can't people think about the marks they leave as they work so hard to make their mark here on earth? So much heartache and trauma could be avoided and systems would not fail, but thrive, if people would just think of others." I said, "I know it sounds silly, but I do feel we are that snowball headed for hell." I asked, "How do I fulfill my childhood passion to help others and follow my father's words to do it right when systems fail and my soul continues to feel the rejection from mankind?" She smiled and said, "You write, they need to know they are not alone, you are not alone, we all get tired." In what would have taken me hours to say, the other part of me punched it out in one line.

The next morning the sun rose and with her came her sister, hope. A young buck blessed me in the early morning hours and even looked up at me as I stood motionless so as not to interrupt his thoughts of being safe. Today mankind was nowhere near these woods. A vibration in my coat pocket told me I was still somewhat connected to mankind. I let it go to voicemail and listened to it from my perch. The voice said I had taught him several years ago and he needed to get his friend to the nonprofit center I volunteer at. I responded to the man with a text, told him that I was hunting and I would connect him to the nonprofit. The man texted back that what I had taught him helped him get through the death of his wife and four weeks later the death of his dog. He also texted, "if not for you, I am not sure where I would be today." As if the sky opened up and God threw a bone to me in the tree top of my perch, I realized that my childhood passion to help others is still out there, even though I feel I'm not contributing like I should. Maybe I had succeeded.

I woke my oldest son up and said, "You told me to wake you up to go hunting, do you still want to go?" He said, "I know it's the last morning of the season and you always hunt in the swamp by yourself, but I really want to kill a deer with a bow this year." I said, "Buddy, this is about you now not me. Let's go." The weather was unusually cold, so after three hours and a half dozen hand and toe warmers I suggested we go down to our cabin and warm up. Our cabin has no running water or electricity and we like that. I turned on the propane heater and warmed up some chicken soup and hot green tea. I could feel the swamp calling me, but I could also feel the moment between a father and son. Over the years, my system of being in the woods has adjusted and improved. Like the deer trails on my family farm, my boys are learning the trail to belonging, inner peace, and a place to process away from mankind. We are finding a place where we gather with the best that God has to offer, a place where moments do not make a mark, just a memory. A place I call my church.

The last evening of deer season went by fast and the walk back to the Jeep was long. A part of me was sad, but the pain was gone. It is late now, the other part of me is sleeping on her left side and the snowballs are safe. I sit here behind the machine that man has created so I can type these words to you, the strangers that know me well, and the ones we have never met, just like the missing man. As I head down the hallway, the magic man lays there right in the way. Most nights he can be found there, waiting for me to pet him or protecting what matters at the end of the hallway—the snowballs and the other part of me. I kneel down, pick his head up from the floor, and hold it in my hands. I kiss him on the side of his nose and he returns with a wet kiss to my face. He does have magic. The hallway has a closet on both sides. My hunting gear is stored in one closet and the other closet is a safe place for items that I have collected along this trail of life. I open this closet and behind my Marine Corps uniform is an old leather jacket. I smell the leather and feel the worn hide. When the quarry rejected my dad, somehow, he and mom found seventy-five dollars to buy an old used motorcycle jacket and a used motorcycle helmet for me as a high school graduation gift. A few years after they gave it to me, the helmet was stolen off my Harley, but the jacket survived. I am not sure where they found seventy-five dollars, but they did, and the jacket is from a moment in time when the system failed my dad, but he did not fail his son. My oldest son wore it a few months ago to a school dance and I told him the story of the jacket.

Like many things we carry and like many things that mark a special place, this jacket may hang in a closet, but it's much more than a jacket. The jacket represents a moment in time that my family tried to forget, but I try to remember, now that I'm the man who has felt the disappointment of mankind. I do my best to make sure that the concrete of life does not surround me. While the trees and the woods comfort me, the jacket is a reminder that I will survive the journey along the trail and the snowballs will survive too. The jacket is not something I carry, but wear as a badge of honor from the man who left behind a healthy child who is now an adult. At the end of the hallway is the only picture in the hallway. The picture is of our second dog, Pascha. A quote from Walt Whitman surrounds her picture; "I bequeath myself to the dirt to grow from the grass I love, if you want me again look for me under your boot-soles." Pascha rests in our backyard and a concrete statue marks the spot where she had her last moment here, and yes, she too had magic.

As I crawl into bed, the wind has stopped blowing and the trees are still. Now that deer season is over, the hooks I had screwed into the trees, to hold my back pack, rifle or bow, have been removed, leaving holes which have now begun the process of healing. The sap will fill and cover the holes and yes, mankind was there in a tree, but the tree will heal and live another day.

Dad accepted two rounds of cancer and never asked "why me," but he never accepted the rejection from the quarry. He never accepted the moment mankind let him down. Most moments in life are about accepting the moment and then accepting the outcome. I struggle with my thoughts that mankind is a snowball headed for hell and pray that my snowballs will follow the trail that I'm making. There will be more days where I lose hope and wish others would think more about how they make their mark versus the mark they make (at others' expense). We all carry things in our backpacks, we all feel pain, even those that seem to have the magic.

- WLV -

Jeff Mitchell & Wm. Josey Visnovske

The Warmth of Love

The word jacket is derived from the French word, 'jaquette' meaning short or small cover. In the English language, there are numerous ways to use the word 'jacket.' Almost all of them describe a jacket as a cover that provides protection to whatever it encloses. A jacket, for example, is the name given to the metal casing that protects the powder in certain bullets. A wiring jacket provides protection to the enclosed wires and keeps them from being chaffed or cut. Librarians are familiar with book jackets that protect hardback books. A file folder that contains several documents is often called a jacket. Another way to use the word jacket is what most people think of when they hear the word. A jacket is an article of outer clothing that provides warmth and protection from wind, cold, rain, and snow. In most cases the Jacket covers from the neck to the waist.

It is apropos that Josey entitled this story as 'The Jacket.' (French lesson # 2. The French word 'apropos' means appropriate, fitting, correct, or just right). The whole story is really a jacket. It covers its contents, that is, many subs-stories within the larger story. Some people call this 'stories within a story.' Josey is very good at writing stories with a story.

In 'The Jacket,' Josey starts, as he often does, with a story from his youth. This one was of him being a teenager and his dad is about to lose his job because of union management conflict. It is a sub-story of family love and loyalty and a willingness to sacrifice for each other. In the main story his parents buy him a leather jacket and a helmet to protect him when he is riding his motorcycle. It was a considerable expense for them when times were hard. The Jacket is a story of maturing and trying to carry some of the burden his family was bearing. In that sub-story we see that Josey gets a strong dose of what psychological trauma is all about when his dad became hurt, dejected and resentful because people he trusted didn't do the right thing and stand up for loyal employees.

The next story within the story depicts a family visit to his wife's aunt who is slowly dying of cancer. Josey has grown very close to Aunt Kathy. She has suffered much trauma in her own life. He teaches his boys the value of experiencing love from this elderly woman even if her time with them is short. When he thinks back on times when he was not doing so well, he also reflects back on the words of his dad, "Son, somebody has it worse."

In other stories within the story, Josey tells tales of hunting with his boys and telling them stories of hunts with his dad, and hunting on Christmas morning. Then Josey speaks of working with people who do the same kind of work he does and the friendship, trust, and loyalty he shares with them.

Josey helps us to understand that we, the people we love as well as the strangers we meet, will all have rough times and times when we all fail. His dad warned him that not everything works out in life. For all of us the message is that it is okay to be temporarily depressed and distressed, but we have to find a way to recover for our sake and for those we know, love, and care for.

In summary, The Jacket and its sub-stories is a story that tells us that to stay mentally and physically healthy we need relationship to loved ones, family and friends. We need to give as well as receive in these relationships of friendship, love, loyalty, care and support. Life is like a jacket protecting and warming the hearts of the people we love and caring for and encouraging people we meet who need our help.

In the story of The Jacket and in these comments Josey and I both wish for you:

Jeff Mitchell & Wm. Josey Visnovske

"That peace on earth fills up your time

That Brotherhood surrounds you

That you may know the warmth of love

and wrap it all around you."

- John Denver, American Folk Singer, from the song 'A Baby Just Like You' by John Denver and Joe Henry, released 1975. Warner/ Chappell Music, Inc.

– JTM –

Story 12

The Manual

Fourteen years ago, when I received the call that Dad had cancer, I had no clue how to react. Several different law enforcement agencies had taught me how to react to various situations, but none had prepared me for this.

Dad survived his first round of cancer and learned of his own mortality. He took the time to do more things he wanted and loved to do, when before, he was too busy to do those things. I took Dad turkey hunting for the first time in his life after he was cured from the first cancer. We did not kill a bird, but I recall that morning like it was yesterday.

The second cancer came back to Dad a few years later and made its mark. It left Dad with limited use of both legs. He was placed into Hospice care, and given a few months to live. Dad's mental, physical, and emotional state changed every year that he lived with the cancer. I knew the dad I had growing up, but then I learned to love and accept the dad who suffered and endured the pain from cancer and all the surgeries. Dad somehow survived the card he had been dealt and graduated from Hospice. I can recall the dad who would take too much pain medication and fall asleep at the kitchen table. I can recall the dad who would not take enough pain meds so the muscles in his face would tighten from the pain.

The second cancer changed Dad from day to day. I can recall the days he would be somewhat happy and then the days that he would be a hateful man.

Following the second cancer was the heart attack, the broken hip, and all the issues related to his colostomy. Dad refused to give into his limited mobility, pain, and poor quality of life.

He would still pull himself onto the tractor and work in the field. He would still fish in his pond, change the oil in his truck, and try his best to be a dad, husband, and friend, despite the pain inside.

One fall, Dad had a surgery to make his colostomy better, but complications arose from that, and he was once again handed the card. He had two close calls in ICU and both times, I waited for the call from Mom. Somehow, he handed the card back and graduated once again. Soon, Dad had more complications. He discovered that years of blood not properly flowing into his lower legs had caused his legs to decay. Dad was sent home in March, placed into Hospice care and given the card once again.

I had moved away from my home state two years before Dad got cancer the first time. I had many conversations with Dad over the years about moving back to help around our small farm, but Dad always said, "You have your life to live." My wife and I, and our two sons, returned to my home state in March after Dad was sent home. We stayed there for a week and tried to spend time with him, but he just slept a lot. My young sons asked about the smell (rotten flesh) that came from Dad's bed. My Mom, who had transformed from a wife to a caregiver years ago, was scared and tired. We did our best to make our visit meaningful and comforting, but it was hard. Dad was going to die this time.

I spoke to my employers, who were more than happy to allow me the freedom to stay with Mom and Dad for a week, and go back and forth as necessary, until Dad died. The ride, every other week, was 13 hours one way. The ride to Mom and Dad's was tough. I knew Mom could not wait for me to get there, but it was hard to watch Dad suffer more and die slowly.

I always thought that Dad would fall into the pond, fall off the tractor, get his wheel chair stuck in the field, and die right there; not die in bed, not my dad. My wife Googled the dying process so we could have some idea of what to expect, and to know what was going on, but there is no Googling the flux of emotions that runs through your head when your dad is dying in front of you. The guilt we felt for the times missed and the anger we felt as he fought to stay with us and our fight to stay awake from being worn out was overwhelming and exhausting. You also feel anger and frustration towards family and friends who cannot bear to see this man in his final moments. And, there is guilt in trying to balance the needs of your immediate family with what is right, what is needed, and what needs to be done.

Dad never had much to say about anything. As the days passed by, Hospice wanted to make sure Dad understood that this was it. He was dying. As the Grim Reaper of Death approached, I sat with my father and explained to him that he was dying. I explained that he could not have his legs amputated due to his poor health and odds were he would die in this bed. He never said a word, but for the first time in my 42 years of living, I saw my dad cry. Mom comforted him, and so did the Hospice nurse, but I left the room and found my peace in the field behind the house.

For fourteen years, every time the caller ID would display Mom and Dad's number, I would cringe. When I would hear Dad's voice, I would breathe a sigh of relief that he was alive. I would accept the man he was that day, maybe not my pre-cancer Dad, but still my dad. On that Sunday morning, Mom called and said he was gone. Once again that flux of emotions; anger, sadness, happiness, guilt, and relief. I did shed a few tears, but not enough to wet my face.

One never thinks about what you are supposed to do on the day your dad dies. Do you sit at the house? Go to church? I decided we should take our boat out and go to the river. Some of my best memories with Dad were on a smaller river with a smaller boat, but water is water.

The next day I loaded up my boys and drove to my home state. My wife wanted to go, but I told her that Mom needed to be a full time mom again. The ride was long and the drive down Mom and Dad's driveway was longer. Dad wanted to be cremated with no service, "no nothing," as he put it. A close friend of mine flew into town to make us laugh, and he did. We spent the week doing things that we could not do because Dad was not able to do them. Dad had left me the combination to his gun safe, and we hoped that maybe this man, who had very little to say, would have left some words of wisdom or wishes. I opened the gun safe to find a few firearms, his dog tags, the five-dollar watch from his 30 years in the rock quarry, a few pictures of mom in her younger years, and some papers, but no wisdom or wishes.

Mom said she would like to have a memorial service for Dad, and I said that would be okay. On a day of remembrance for our nation, September 11th, we celebrated the short, painful life of my dad. Dad was too sick the day I marched across the parade deck of Parris Island, so on this day, I wore my Marine Corps uniform. My brother was there with his family, but my sister did not come. My Mom looked at me at one point and asked me if I wanted to say something about Dad, but I declined. Once again, that flux of emotions ran through me; anger, sadness, happiness, guilt, and relief. How does one address a group of people and state, "I'm so relieved he is dead?"

A month after Dad died, I sat at my rifle-shooting bench on my friend's farm. It's a place you can find me at least three days a week. It's my alcohol, golf, and therapist. It's my way to connect the dots of life. The rifle in front of me is one I've had since I was a teenager. A few years ago, I amazed my dad when I taped a quarter to a post and shot a hole through it at 100 yards. I took the quarter and made a necklace for Dad. Dad added a few religious medals to it and wore it in the final years until it wore into his skin. Then it was placed on the triangle thing that hung above his bed. Thinking of him that day on the farm, I taped a quarter at 100 yards and concentrated on what needed to be done. I took a few shots and knew I hit the quarter, but to my surprise, I put two holes through it. I cried enough tears to wet my face and then some. This time the emotion was purely missing my dad.

I would imagine that somewhere out there is a book that will tell you how to navigate through the flux of emotions that are experienced when you find yourself in these waters. I titled this letter as The Manual because I wanted to share the above, in hopes that it will help you when you find yourself in this boat.

One time I told my dad that I did not get my sister and he said, "Its ok. She does not get you." I learned from the above experience that we are all different. Some of us can handle situations, and some can't. My brother never helped much with Dad, but he is who he is. My sister helped some, but has her moments when she is not that solid. Just because I made the journey does not make me the better child, I'm just geared different.

I can tell you that the flux of emotions is a roller coaster, a boat flume, a parachute; a ride like no other. At times your senses are on overload and you really want to be numb for a while, to take a break, but you can't, you are needed.

I can tell you that the things you receive from the living are much better than the things that are left for you when they die. My dad's deer rifle feels good in my hands and feels even better when I use it, because he personally handed it to me as a gift. The firearms he left in the gun safe for me remind me my dad is gone. My dad's gun safe sits in my shop now and I will fill it with wishes and wisdom, so those who are left behind will not wonder.

I have graduated from five separate law enforcement academies and one boot camp, but there is no training like that I received from March to August of that year. I would never want to endure it again, but I will be better at everything I do because I witnessed, lived, suffered, and helped my dad die.

I can tell you that one of the finest organizations that our country has to offer is Hospice. The doctors, nurses, and social workers are a special and unique group of people. They are somehow able to endure, day and night, helping those who were handed the card and the families that watch them die.

If you live long enough, you will lose someone you know or love to cancer; it does not discriminate. Cancer slowed my dad down and we became closer because of it. Cancer slowed my dad down so he would play Barbie's with my sister's daughter. Cancer taught us the meaning of real pain.

Death somehow brings us together or reunites us for a short moment. It reintroduces us to old heroes we looked up to. Death reminds us that this ride is short and we should never take that short span of time for granted. The year of his death was the fastest in my life and the longest for my dad. Dad had trouble being a grandpa to my boys due to the pain. I remember him saying "I can't be the grandpa I want to be." Death somehow bonded my oldest son to my dad and now they seem to be connected in a way I don't understand, but I'm glad.

I'm not sure if Dad taught me this or if it just came naturally, but no matter what you do when you find yourself in these waters, just do what you can. You will never truly grasp or control the flux of emotions. You will have regrets, you will wish for one more moment with that someone. You will feel anger, sadness, happiness, guilt, and relief more than once. In March of that year, a friend told me that when the final card is handed to you all, "You have to take care of your dad, it is the only way your boys will learn that's what you do when someone needs you." My friend's words rang in my ears more than once as I made that 13-hour ride.

A few months after Dad died, my friend, who owns the farm where I shoot, suddenly became sick and died within a few days. As his family gathered around his hospital bed to watch him die, I felt all those same emotions again. Every time I walked into the hospital room I could see those same emotions in their faces. It doesn't matter if its a few days, weeks, or months, the emotions are all the same. My friend lay there, just like Dad had, and all I could do was wait. My friend was buried on a Sunday, and that night, using the headlights of my truck, I shot his targets that I had set up for him at his favorite pond on the farm. The next day, I placed a quarter at 100 yards and, with a few practice shots I placed one round through the quarter. My ceremony of shooting may not be conventional, but it's my way of showing those that I love and cared for that I can still stay focused on the task at hand despite the pain in my heart just like watching them die.

My dad used to tell everyone when he would part paths with them, "It's a jungle out there." Dad was right, it is a jungle with this thing called Google, when we want to know something. I don't think Google, a therapist, a priest, or a bottle of alcohol can help one navigate through the death of a loved one, but we can help each other. There were many who helped me as I traveled the road between my home here, and Mom and Dad's house. I recall one particular night staying at a friend's house and I hugged him and said, "Thanks." He said, "No, thank you, I'm getting more out of this than you." At the time, his words made no sense to me, but now I understand. We all get something out of a situation, but we may not realize it at the time due to the flux of emotions. My dad experienced pain for fourteen years, but somehow still had the will to live another day. Those of us that watched and experienced the many faces and personalities of Dad's last fourteen years know and understand that life is not perfect, just like us. I've often said that watching someone you love, die from cancer, can emotionally infect the people who love that person and it can 'eat them alive.' I sometimes wish the cancer would have passed my dad up and found someone else, but who would wish that on anyone? I do believe there is a "plan." It may not make sense to me now, but the waters I'm in at this moment don't allow me the time to figure out the plan. I have to do what is right, what is needed, and what needs to be done.

Semper FI

Written by a man whose dad and a good friend died in the same year.

- WLV -

Story 13

The Jukebox

As my wife and I bounced down the dirt-logging road between the planted pines, I parked the Jeep and said, "We will have to walk from here." I made sure I had the quart glass Mason jar in my backpack and grabbed my rifle. I told her it was not a far walk and, as she rubbed her belly, she said, "I need the exercise." As we made our way into the swamp, I could tell the last rain we had was still with us. The ground was wet and I had to look ahead to avoid the pockets of water. We walked over to the creek and saw that the creek was too high for us to cross with our rubber boots. I told my wife that there was a large pine, a little further down, that had blown over in a storm that we could use to cross the creek. She smiled and said, "Sounds good."

The pine was so big that I could not wrap my arms around it and while it still had some green in the needles, the tree was dying. I climbed up onto the pine and helped my wife up. I asked, "Are you sure you are ok with crossing the creek this way?" She replied, "I'm pregnant not broken." I took a few steps and turned around just in time to see her slip and fall. She landed on her back as she splashed into the water. I jumped into the creek to help her. She came up from the water, stood up in about waist deep water and said, "That was refreshing." We stood waist deep in the creek and between us was all that mattered, our first child.

She assured me she was fine, but I took off my Marine Corps sweatshirt to keep her warm. The water was not that cold, but she looked cold. I told her we would head home and she said, "No, we came here for a reason." As we got out of the creek, we walked to a spot where the swamp necks down and I said,

"This is it." I took off my backpack, removed the glass Mason jar, and filled it with swamp water. As I tightened the lid she asked, "Are you sure Father John will let us baptize our first child with swamp water?" I said, "Once I told him about the magical healing powers that the swamp has for me, he said yes, but to boil the swamp water first." As we walked back to the Jeep, we laughed at how bad this could have looked for a husband who took his pregnant wife to the swamp and then got injured. No one would believe it was just an accident.

It was 4:30 a.m. and my alarm was due to go off in an hour, but I lay there and stared at the ceiling. Today was a day that I had hoped and prayed for, but I had also lived in fear of its arrival. My wife lay there because she was tired as it had been a long week. I got out of bed, the boys were asleep, and I eased their door shut. As I made my way down the hallway, I saw our dog lying there waiting on me, his best friend. I took a knee, held his head up off the floor, and massaged his ears. I made biscuits and gravy, and waffles for the boys and left them on the kitchen counter.

Before the sun broke through the pine trees across the field, I was headed 12 miles up the road to check on a hog trap. The classic country radio station took me back to a place that was miles from here, and on this day, I needed to remember those simpler days. It was the first day of bow season and I needed to be in the woods for a little while today, but I did not have enough time to bow hunt this morning. I pulled into the cotton field and grabbed the same rifle that I had on that day my wife took a dip in the creek. The rifle has more marks on it now, but so do I. As I worked my way along the cotton field I could see all of the hog tracks at the edge of the field. To some, the wild hog is not a problem, but to the American farmer, it is the beast that lurks in the darkness waiting to destroy their crops. I checked the hog trap.

The sun was now up, and it shined down with hope that today would be a good day. I texted my wife from the cotton field that I would be home soon and we could leave after I took a quick shower. The ride home was long and my heart was already beating faster than the music on the radio but it did not calm my nerves.

I got my Wrangler jeans, boots, and a button down shirt from the closet. My wife asked, "That's what you are wearing?" I replied, "She told me to dress comfortable so this is comfortable." I pulled my belt buckle from the dresser drawer and my wife asked, "You wearing the big one today?" I said, "Yes, it belonged to Gary and today I need him." My wife left the bedroom and I reached into the back of the dresser drawer and grabbed an old red handkerchief that belonged to my dad. He always carried one in his pocket.

My oldest son greeted me in the kitchen and asked, "Are you sure its ok if I do not go?" I said, "It's ok." My wife, my youngest son, and I loaded up into the truck and drove the 25 miles to town. The classic country station continued to play, but no amount of music or memories could slow down my heart. I called a farmer and talked to him about the hogs on his farm just to stop my mind from racing. We normally laugh and carry on in the truck, but today the tension is thick.

As I pulled into the parking lot, the reality sets in. This day has come. A tear burst from behind my sunglasses and the show has not even started yet. I grabbed my 11-year old's hand and we all walked to the front door. My cowboy boots struck the asphalt like a hammer nailing in nails. As we walked in the door, a man said, "You can sit wherever." I swallowed hard and another tear burst from my eye as I said, "I'm an honorary pallbearer." The man said, "Wait here and I will take you and the others up in a bit." My mouth was dry, my heartbeat was faster, and the tears came. My son squeezed my hand and looked up at me confused. I looked down and said, "This is hard for daddy, but I will be ok." My wife of 22 years knows that a pat on the back will not help me at this point. I'm like a limb falling to the ground and it has to fall before you can pick it up. The man soon returned so I followed him and the others to the front of the church; and there he laid, my friend.

In my left hand were my collection of dog tags and medals where my sweat has already found a home around them. The world and my friend can now see my eyes, which were watered and red. I fought the tears and then the anger came with intense force. I know how my friend ended up here. I know more about his life than most. I tried to help him, but he was gone way before we ever met. I searched for him, but I never found him. His mom called me a few days ago and said, "I had always hoped it would have been you that found him." I said, "I know, but I'm pretty sure he found me."

As I waited for the service to begin, I drifted deep into the past and thought about things that I had buried, just like someone buried him. As I unearthed the raw, distorted emotions, I went from sad to angry. I pulled the red handkerchief from my pants pocket and wiped my eyes. I thought of my father's words, "Do it right or do not do it at all." In the short time that I looked for my friend, I knew I did it right, but wondered if I could have done more.

I saw movement in the front corner of the church and there was his mom being pushed in a wheel chair. It had been years since I had seen her. The 18 years her son was lost had worn on her. If only I had found him, maybe, the 18 years could have been 8 years. She smiled and waved at me as the people stood up when the family entered the church. Her wheel chair was parked right in front of the box that now held the remains of her lost son. In life, we should all have a job that we do, but what's more important is that we do our part. The sight of her and the lost son so close together did not comfort me like I thought it would. Instead, it was proof that this time, my part was not enough.

A man got up and spoke of my friend's childhood, which seemed to mirror mine. The first time I met his mom she said, "You are just like my son that is missing." My left hand rubbed all the dog tags and medals on my collection just like I had seen many people do, but never me. My mind continually drifted into that hole where I guess I buried the failure I felt when I was not the one who walked across her yard to say, "We found him."

The day they found him and unearthed his remains was the day the shallow grave of my distorted emotions came to light. The man stopped speaking and then the preacher man spoke. To be honest, what can you say in a situation like this? I rubbed my collection and prayed for strength from those who have contributed to it. Some are living, some are dead, but they all seem to be with me. It is all I can do to look at his mom. I feel ashamed and guilty that I did not do more, but she praises me every time we speak.

The music and talking has stopped, the funeral man looked at me as our cue to get up and leave this place. As my boots struck the carpet between the isles, my head was low. The tears flowed from my eyes and like an egg-sucking dog (a dog that eats the eggs in a chicken house and tries to sneak out) I wanted to leave this place. The funeral man told us to stand next to the hearse as the pallbearers loaded the coffin. I stood there not feeling like I deserved a position of honor. The funeral man told us that we could go inside where it was cool and stand next to the missing man's mom as she greeted people when they left the church.

I walked into the church and there she sat in that damn wheel chair. I knelt down and the retainer wall inside of me broke as I hugged her. I repeatedly said, "I'm sorry." I stood up with the others and felt that I had no business here. I interrupted the line of people and told the missing man's mom that I would be outside standing next to her son. At the corner of the hearse, I stood, big belt buckle and all. The sun beat down and soon the sweat rolled down my back. Finally, after all the years of searching, I could stand with my friend and do for him what I had failed to do many years ago. People looked at me when they left the church. I am not sure if they understood why I was standing there. My sunglasses hid my quivering eyes and my heart beat like that hammer driving those nails.

My youngest son came down the steps and wrapped his arms around my waist and another retainer wall broke inside me. My son started to cry and asked, "Daddy, why are you standing out here?" I said, "He was alone for a long time and today he will not lay out here and be alone." My wife came down the steps, my tears flowed more, and she hugged me. She knew why I was standing there and she knew that an earthquake would not make me leave my friend. A lawyer man walked up and hugged me. I knew him and knew his father. His father was a lawman and a Marine. The lawyer man said, "Thanks for being here. How are you?" I said, "Not doing so good today." The lawyer man said, "Don't give up, we need people like you out here in this world doing what you do." The lawyer man knew that years ago when I failed to find my friend I almost quit my job.

The church had emptied and soon the missing man's mom rolled by in her wheel chair. I stood there motionless with my wife and son by my side. The parking lot was empty except for the few cars in line behind the black limo. As the missing man's mom got into the back seat, the funeral man looked over at me and nodded that I could go. We never discussed my self-appointed position, but I think to most it was clear what I was doing, especially to the funeral man.

We drove to the cemetery and once again, the country classic station did not slow down my beating heart. As we walked down the drive to the gravesite, my boots struck the asphalt with more intensity than in the church. The tears for the moment had stopped and now I was angry. I could not tell what I was angry at, but the anger was deep inside me. I stepped back away from the small crowd and chose to stand in the sun. I could see the missing man's mom and in front of her was the coffin. The funeral man walked up on my left. I turned my head. He reached up and touched my shoulder. My wife and son stood by my side, but, to be honest, all I could see and feel was the missing man and his mom. It was as if we were the only ones there. The preacher man spoke, but I heard none of it. The small crowd of people moved about which told me the show was over.

One by one, people bent over and spoke to the missing man's mom. Out of the corner of my eye, a man approached and introduced himself as the missing man's uncle. He asked who I was and I told him, with tears rolling down my face. He said, "Thank you for all you have done for our family." The tears flowed harder and all I could say was, "Yes Sir" and "Yes Sir." He realized at that moment that I was broken and said, "Thanks again." As he walked away, two women came up and introduced themselves as the missing man's aunts. I hugged them both and said, with tears on my face, "I'm sorry." Once again, all I could say was "Yes ma'am" and "Yes ma'am." Their praise and thanks landed in a place deep within me that was filled with shame and guilt for not finding their nephew.

I saw that the line of people to the missing man's mom was now done so my time had come. I walked over, but my boots felt like they were sinking in the grass. I knelt down and hugged her. All the retainer walls broke and she held me as I cried. She said, "Do you have any peace with this?" I said, "No." She said, "Nor do I." I told her I was angry and sad and the emotions bounced backed and forth since I walked into the church. She said, "My son is angry and you are his voice here. My son will not be at peace until justice is served." She held me in her arms and I realized that the grieving mother was comforting me, the man who had never met her son. I was the man who came along and was asked to help find her son - the man who failed to find him.

I reached into my shirt pocket and pulled out a USMC key chain with a bullet hole in it. I told the missing man's mom that I shot it for her the night before. She said, "Thank you." I pulled out from my shirt pocket a quarter with a bullet hole in it and said, "This is for your son and it needs to go in the hole with him." The funeral man was sitting behind the missing man's mom and said, "Follow me." We walked over to the coffin and he raised the flowers that were laying on top it and said, "Stick the quarter in the crack right there." I said, "Ok, but I need a minute" and he walked away.

I laid my hands on the coffin, the anger came, but so did the intense sadness. I made a fist with my right hand and wanted to punch the coffin, but realized that was not the answer. I put both hands back on the coffin and stood there with weak legs and a weak heart. I cried, I cussed inside, and yes, the pain was indescribable. How could I have these emotions for a man I had never met? How could this pain be more than when I lost my dad? Why the hell am I here? At that moment, it was just my friend and I at the gravesite. It was as if the world did not exist. I raised the flowers, saw the crack the funeral man had showed me, and inserted my shot quarter. It was as if this was the jukebox of life, as if a song would emerge from the earth under us and the earth where he spent the last 18-years, that would explain it to me,   and explain it to us all.

I walked away from the coffin and never said a word to anyone. My wife and son soon figured out that the show was over, and it was time to go home. As my boots struck the asphalt, I said to my wife, "That sucked." I had little to say on the way home. The classic country station brought me some peace, but at one point, I looked at my wife and said, "I'm numb."

I knew the time after the funeral would be rough so I made plans for our family to drive about 40 miles to help a farmer with a hog problem. We stopped at the house, changed clothes, picked up our oldest boy and started driving. As we drove the truck there, I had the windows down and the classic country station playing loud. Even if someone wanted to talk, it would have been hard with the music and wind noise. We crossed a river and my wife yelled to the boys sitting in back, "See if you see any boats."

That was the river we went to the day my mom called and told me that dad died. I thought back to that day, but the pain I felt today was much worse than that day. We drove about another ten miles, we crossed another river, and soon we found ourselves in the company of a farmer, his wife, and their teenage son. After about a twenty-minute drive down into the woods, we were in an area where the hogs had started to destroy the land. We helped them set up a trap and explained what we knew about the behavior of hogs. From time to time, my mind would drift back to the cemetery and then all the pain would return. As the sun set, we loaded up to come home, and the farmer walked over to our truck and said, "Thanks. And, you all got some hard working polite young men. You all are doing a great job of raising them."

The ride home was dark and my wife and boys were tired. I was still numb, but as the woods left us and the pavement rolled under our tires, the reality of my friend set in. We crossed the first bridge and then 10 miles later we crossed the second bridge. The sound of hollow concrete under our tires made me remember how I felt 10 years ago when I had done my part, but had to stop looking for my friend. I struggled so much with it that I went to see a psychologist and sat on her sofa. After she asked me if I drank, if I was abusive to my wife and kids, and a whole series of other questions, all of which I answered "No ma'am" to, she said, "Then what's the problem?" I told her that I was on a bridge and I could not get across it. I can see the other side, but I'm stuck there. I cannot get this guy that I never met out of my head. She said, "I'm not sure what to do for you." I appreciated her honest answer because most of us would rather have the truth than a load of crap. I went back to her a few more times and one of those times handed her a story I wrote called, "Did you see anything." She sat in front me, read it and soon tears flowed from her eyes. I guess she realized I had an outlet for what ailed me even though she could not help me cross the bridge. After the psychologist, I retreated to my woods where I would sit on my perch and cried more than I care to say. I never wrote about my friend, but a keen soul can find him buried in the lines of many stories over the last ten years. I stopped seeing his mom just because I felt so bad in that I could no longer help look for her son. No written words can describe the amount of guilt I felt for not finding him and not staying by her side.

As we pulled into the driveway, it's good to be home, but the memory of my friend is here. A deer head hangs on the wall from a deer I had killed on one of many anniversary dates from the day he went missing. I wiped tears from my eyes that morning as the deer came into site and then I shot it. I doubt my family knows that about the deer, but I do every time I pass it. I crawl into bed and pray for the peace of night or that maybe work will call and I can feel the comfort from a coworker who does not know what I did today. Many around me know of this story, but not in this detail.

The night was peaceful, but I was exhausted. My youngest son was up with me the next morning as I made breakfast and I asked, "Do you know why daddy was so upset yesterday?" As he kicked his feet around the kitchen floor and started to say this and that he finally said, "No." I told him our job in life is to protect others, to help others, and to do the right thing, and to do your part. Daddy tried hard to find that man, but I couldn't and daddy just feels bad inside. My youngest son said with a nervous smile, "I understand daddy" and he hugged me. I was ready to start my day when the first phone call came. The same friend who called me to tell me they found the missing man was now checking on me. We talked for a good hour and even though he did not have the answers, he listened. I had to laugh inside at me rubbing the collection of dog tags and medals in the church and now a friend holding the door open for me so I could catch my breath. We all struggle for our next breath, even those of us that seem to have all the answers.

I walked into the house after talking to my friend and my family looked at me, but not like they normally do. Then my ears heard the song playing that I've heard a hundred times, "I'm going to live forever" by Billy Joe Shaver. I stopped like I was nailed to the floor and heard the line, "I'm going to cross that river." I froze in time and listened to every word in the song. I had never listened to every word before.

I'm gonna live forever
I'm gonna cross that river
I'm gonna catch tomorrow now
You're gonna wanna hold me
Just like I've always told you
You're gonna miss me when I'm gone

Transition Man

Nobody here will ever find me
But I will always be around
Just like the songs I leave behind me
I'm gonna live forever now
You fathers and you mothers
Be good to one another
Please try to raise your children right
Don't let the darkness take 'em
Don't make 'em feel forsaken
Just lead 'em safely to the light

When this old world is blown asunder
And all the stars fall from the sky
Remember someone really loves you
We'll live forever you and I

- Billy Joe Shaver / Eddy (John Edwin) Shaver (1993)
"I'm Gonna Live Forever" – Live Forever Lyrics,
Universal Music Publishing Group, Warner / Chappell
Music Inc. -

At that moment, I felt peace and the anger was gone. I felt me cross the bridge that I had been stuck on for years. I saw my hand stick that quarter into the coffin, the jukebox of life that gave me a song that brought me, and I am sure my lost friend, some peace.

It has been a few days since we buried my friend and I have never written about something so soon after it happened, but this story has been in the hole way too long. This story hangs from almost every limb where I retreat for peace. This story is part of my story. There are many unanswered questions as to why a man I had never met made such a huge impact on my life. A friend of mine is a Choctaw Indian. He told me that his people believe when a warrior is killed, the warrior will seek the spirit of another warrior to make it right. I guess my friend felt safe telling me that because he knows I am part Cherokee.

Most who know me well realize that being in the woods is where I am at peace with the earth. Sitting Bull defined a warrior in this manner:

"For us, warriors are not what you think of as warriors. The warrior is not someone who fights, because no one has the right to take another's life. The warrior, for us, is one who sacrifices himself for the good of others. His task is to take care of the elderly, the defenseless, those who cannot provide for themselves, and above all, the children, the future of humanity."

> – Sitting Bull,1831-1890 (Hunkpapa Lakota leader who defended and protected Lakota people against unfair and illegal US government policies that allowed an invasion of gold prospectors and settlers who confiscated sacred native American lands.)

I never knew that was the definition of a warrior until I wrote this story. In the short time that I physically spent looking for my lost friend, I too became lost inside myself as I looked for him. For years, I had buried those distorted emotions in a hole only for them to become unearthed the day we gave him the burial he had earned as a warrior. I stood by my friend's side, at the back of the hearse, because he was too defenseless to care for himself. As I stood at his coffin and inserted a part of me, the coin, into that crack, to forever protect my friend, who I never met, I thought that was the love of a fellow warrior.

Yes, there are many unanswered questions in this story, but it has taken me 10 years, and him 18 years to get here. The jukebox of life has brought us peace. Yes, there is still pain, but not the anger that I felt that day. A hole shot quarter, a crack in a coffin, crossing two rivers, and an old classic country song may all be a coincidence, or could be me looking to the sky for answers, or me trying to cope, or maybe it's the spirit of a warrior telling his fellow warrior that you did more than your part.

– WLV –

Jeff Mitchell & Wm. Josey Visnovske

Persistence

"Consciously or not, we are all on a quest for answers, trying to learn the lessons of life. We grapple with fear and guilt. We search for meaning, love, and power. We try to understand fear, loss, and time. We seek to discover who we are and how we can become truly happy."

> - Elisabeth Kubler-Ross, (1926-2004) Swiss-American Psychiatrist, Author of the landmark book, 'On death and Dying'

The 'Jukebox' begins with a tender love story between Josey and his wife and their unborn child. That is a special moment-in-time kind of story, one that touches anyone who loves someone. There are many who would be happy for the story to begin and end right there. We should know by now, however, that Josey always has more to tell. Other things happen and his life gets more complicated. Sometimes things of the past creep into his present life. Sometimes new things arise that absorb his attention (as well as ours). So, climb into Josey's time machine and hold on.

Zip forward about a dozen years and Josey gets word that an old case he worked years before has gone from cold to hot. A new lead came from somewhere and a body has finally been uncovered. Despite the fact that he no longer has any responsibility in the case because, for a long time, he has not done that type of law enforcement work, the recovery of a missing man sends him into a whirlwind of emotional reactions.

To be very clear, law enforcement and other emergency personnel are not stirred by every case they encounter or every time they were unable to reach a successful conclusion of a case or situation. No one would be able to psychologically survive if they were impacted by every situation they come across. Most situations pass on by like an express train going through a station without stopping. Every once in awhile though, emergency personnel encounter something that latches onto them and they may latch onto it. These cases may be memorable moments-in-time but of the worst kind.

Why do certain events have sticking power while others do not? There can be many explanations. Perhaps we lived through some personal tragedy in our youth and the current situation is a very powerful reminder of the past personal event. Sometimes we react because we imagine our children caught up in a terrible situation like a victim we are helping now or one we just finished helping. In other cases, our imagination takes over and suggests to us that we could be that person who is suffering before our eyes as we work to help or save them. Sometimes we feel guilty that we arrived too late or that we did not do enough to make a difference. We can also feel guilty about something we failed to do in the past and the current situation brings up reminders of our guilt feelings. Our guilt over our own perceived failures or the circumstances of a tragedy can make us angry. Threat, loss, fear, guilt, anger, vulnerability, perceived weakness, and powerlessness are all powerful emotions that can cause us to freeze up or they may divert us from effective work.

When we are faced with unfinished business from the past, the emotions don't just disappear. They get stored like hazardous materials in storage barrels in our brains. We don't stop thinking of those fragments of things that never came to a conclusion. They are there, lurking in the back alleys of our brains just waiting for a resolution; just waiting for a light to shine on them. We are not always aware of the efforts our brains are making to complete, simplify and categorize all those bits and pieces and the mysteries of our past that have never been resolved. Our brains are always working. In one sense, the work of the brain makes me think of the hum in a florescent light. It is always there, but we need the light and we get absorbed in our daily lives. We don't pay much attention to the ever-present hum. Sometimes, in a quiet moment when we slow down, we notice the hum.

In a similar manner, one day something happens in our world and a mental switch in our brains gets flipped and a mystery gets solved or we are able to connect the dots. That brings a torrent of emotions to the surface. Joy, relief, excitement, happiness, embarrassment, frustration, loss, guilt, anger, sadness, loss, resentment, whatever has been stored, all come out at once. Together, they make a set of powerful emotional reactions. They have all been waiting a long time to burst out of their brainy storage barrels. One result of this sudden release of stored emotions is tears that don't seem to have an end.

In the Jukebox, Josey suddenly experiences a flood of tears that represent an emptying of the emotional hazardous material barrels that have been stored in his brain for over a decade. It is a fair question to ask, "How can someone be so emotionally overwhelmed by the conclusion of an eighteen year old murder case? How can he refer to the missing man, now found, as his friend when he had never met him?"

The answer is two-fold. First, there are hints in the story of the Juke box that indicate that Josey, through his work in the investigation, had come to know more about the missing man than most people who had friendships with the man. Second, Josey developed a strong friendship with the man's mother that lasted long after the case became a cold case and Josey moved onto a new job. Personal attachment became the source of his tears.

"There is a sacredness in tears. They are not the mark of weakness, but of power. They speak more eloquently than ten thousand tongues. They are the messengers of overwhelming grief, of deep contrition, and of unspeakable love."

- Washington Irving (1783-1859), American short story writer, historian and diplomat. Wrote 'The Legend of Sleepy Hollow' and 'Rip Van Winkle'

Everyone's brain is persistent. Brains keep trying to figure it all out. They are relentless in their pursuit of completeness. That being said, not every person is persistent. Not everyone learns persistence as they grow up. As humans grow. They are supposed to learn from parents, teachers and religious leaders to stick to, defend, and protect their families their friends and their country. Children should learn loyalty, integrity, honesty, generosity, love, care and persistence in relationships to others.

Persistence is the inner stuff that keeps us going when life gets tough. It drives people to complete their studies and their projects. It helps people to do tough jobs, to make sacrifices, to pursue every lead and to keep on giving even when it hurts. Persistence does not let us give up even when the odds are stacked against us.

Josey stuck with the case of the missing man. He pursued the case with all of his energy. He never gave up even when the case went cold. He kept the theories about the crime alive in his mind. He stayed loyal to the missing man's mother even when there was nothing more he could do.

Like a soldier standing guard at the tomb of the unknown, Josey kept a silent watch over the casket of his friend, the missing man, so the man would not have to be alone. He did not walk away even when the heat of the sun beat down upon him and his clothes became saturated with sweat. He was persistent.

"Persistent people have a goal or vision in mind that motivates and drives them. They are often dreamers and visionaries who see their lives as having a higher purpose than simply earning a living. Their vision is deeply ingrained, and they focus on it constantly and with great emotion and energy."

- Ashish Janiani, Mumbai, India, Motivational Speaker, Founder of Motivational Diaries

- JTM -

Story 14

Did You See Anything?

A good friend asked me the other day if I had seen anything on my morning hunt. I said, "No," but I felt as though I had lied to him.

Those of you that know me well are aware that my life revolves around deer season. I prepare all year for those five months. The first few weeks of deer season, I hunt hard to fill our freezers with the meat we will need for the year. I stress until our freezers are full because I worry that work will call me away from hunting, that I will get injured and be unable to hunt, or I that will lose the place where I hunt. Once our freezers are filled, I hunt to fill my soul. Let me explain. I am one of those unfortunate people who lets the evilness of society and the ill intentions of man stick to my soul like briars stick to my hunting pants. Once the freezers are full, I retreat to the woods to take in what most people seem to have forgotten; the raw, untouched beauty of nature. In a world of high definition televisions, DVD's, etc., its beauty assures me that there is peace.

The other morning I was sitting in one of my deer stands that about 40 feet above the ground in a pine tree. I had climbed up to the stand while most of you were still in bed. As I sat there in the dark, I recalled the woods below. These are the woods where my dog tracked her last deer some two years ago before she died. I looked to my right and recalled the field where I had killed a doe on a deer hunt with my 3 and a half-year-old son, our second hunt together. I looked to my left and recalled that warm Saturday morning as I was sneaking up on a deer only to find myself crossing paths with a 6-foot rattlesnake that was sneaking up on a squirrel. We came to an agreement where I did not tell the squirrel and he did not tell the deer. As the sun started to break into this dark world, I heard the hogs in the swamp sing their song. The sun is now up and it has found its way to the pines that surround me. I feel it's warmth against my cold feet and the morning has arrived.

Our society has painted a picture of hunting to sell its product. The allure of the big horned beast has made many a hunter. I too have killed a few of the big horned beasts, not for their horns, but for their size because they have more meat for my freezers. I would imagine there are other hunters like me. Hunters who retreat to the woods to visit a society untouched by man, but I wonder if they would admit it in public or share it with strangers.

As I sit here, 40 feet off of the ground on cold days, warm days, and windy days, I can't imagine why anyone would want to watch the game, the fight, the news or anything where you are a spectator. In these woods you are a part of something so big, so much bigger than anything man has created.

The sun is now warming my face and I realize that this gift will soon be over. Unlike the trees that surround me, or the deer that I so admire, I am human and understand time. It's time for me to crawl down from my perch and return to a world of technology. A world that spins so fast, we seem to forget about the beauty that lies in these woods. As I walk back to my Jeep I tell myself it was a good hunt. My soul is filled with images that will carry me through until I return again. As I witness the evils of man or the lack of respect for this world, I will recall these woods and know that there is peace. Sometimes, a good hunt does not always mean the sound of my rifle, the releasing of my bowstring, or a bloody knife. Sometimes, a good hunt is the pure, simple, sound of nothing, the sound of peace, the sound of life without the influence of man.

Days after my friend asked his question I reflected on my answer. I guess I should have said, "I saw everything."

WLV-

Jeff Mitchell & Wm. Josey Visnovske

Story 15

The Loop

As I crossed the creek, I saw the school bus fly by the end of our gravel driveway. I ran back up the hill to tell mom I missed the bus but we could catch it when it came by where the creeks meet. After the bus would pick me up, it went a few more miles down the county gravel road and then got on a two-lane pavement road. After about five miles on the paved road, it turned on a gravel road, which eventually headed back to the gravel road where we lived. The whole time the bus picked up kids for the small Catholic school I went to and it also picked up kids that went to the public school. My mom was not mad that I missed the bus as she drove me to where the creeks meet. I never told her that the reason I missed the bus was because I was throwing rocks in the creek below our house. The bus came to a sliding stop and the dust that followed it covered me for a few seconds. Mr. Schneider, the bus driver, smiled as I got on the bus and then laughed.

As we turned down the gravel road to Aunt Kathy's house the sound of crunching gravel is stored deep inside my head. For the most part, these memoires are good or, maybe I should say, these memories are simple. As we turn into the driveway to Aunt Kathy's house, the red, white and blue flag at the end of the porch brings color to the winter setting that is upon us. Thoughts of the recent Veterans Day mass and reception I attended at my son's Catholic school race through my head and then linger for a moment. The memories are no longer simple but complex. My mom, my wife, and our two boys bail from the truck to embrace the reason we came this great distance. I sit there in that simple and complex state of mind questioning my role here. I wish, at times, I could just live in the moment and not question the purpose of the moment. In a small bag under the truck seat is a collection of dog tags and religious medals that has become my purpose and my role for being here in this moment called life. What is about to embrace us all is the woman who a year and half ago was a distant Aunt of my wife's. Now she, without asking, has become a part of my collection and my purpose.

Our paths met because I put her son in a book I wrote. He was a Blackhawk pilot that died in Iraq. It was then she told me, without a tear in her eye, she was dying. I remember standing there with tears in my eyes as this stranger told me her fate. I felt envy that she has embraced what most of us fear. I have often said that when you die for something you believe in, there is no fear at the moment. Over the 28 years of being a police officer, I have put my life at risk because I believed in the moment I was in. But the fear of death lingers around me when there is no moment, just life. Aunt Kathy has no fear because she has faith in life.

As we make our way to the house, we can see that the front porch is filled with chairs to sit in and one swing where, on the warmer days, you will often find Aunt Kathy. I know, from the journals she has given me to help me write a book on her life, that the rocking and swinging refresh her memories of her grandmother holding her and rocking her. That grandmother is the same one with whom she would say the rosary.

The moment has arrived and the embracing and the meetings begin. The tall thin woman hugs us all. I can feel her bones as I hug her and I do my best not to stay in that moment too long for this is life and I need to embrace it not fear it. On the back porch stands a woman who I do not recognize. She turns and I realize it's the widow of the son killed in Iraq. I met her on a cold day fifteen years ago when they brought him home. I had not seen her since. She walked into the house and hugged me. Her man followed her. Her "man," as I call him, has accepted that the widow calls this place home and the people who live here are her family. The idea that Aunt Kathy's family has accepted her "man" tells me that they too accept that life does not turn out like we plan. As the chatter increases, my mind drifts, as it often does. I watch Aunt Kathy as if a sign will appear from her as to why our paths have crossed. Am I here to write a book on her life? Am I here to help transition her to the next place? Or, maybe, it's not just about her; it's about me.

I rehearsed in my head the things I wanted to ask Aunt Kathy when I saw her next so I continued to rehearse them as I watched her prepare her legendary green beans for the Thanksgiving feast. Her body is rigid as she moves through the kitchen from the many cancer issues that have scarred her. Though she seldom complains of the pain, from where I stand as the silent observer, I cannot only see the pain but I can feel it. She grabs two bottles of the special formula she feeds her stomach and, for the last five years, that has been her Thanksgiving feast as well as every meal she eats.

We all drive in a caravan from Aunt Kathy's house to the cornfield below her house. At the edge of the cornfield sit two houses that mark the homes of two of Aunt Kathy's daughters and their families. In a tree at the first house is a special swing for their daughter who was born with muscular dystrophy. At the age of 16, she can move one finger and that is it. A smile seems to have been painted on her face by God and her soul is lined with the greatest sunrise you will ever see. This family has embraced life and what others see as a problem they see as a blessing.

The second house has no special swing but a concrete ramp signifies that the door is open to all even those who can only move one finger. The chatter in the second house is louder than Aunt Kathy's and I search for a spot to blend in as the silent observer. Uncle Bill stopped my efforts by finding me a spot and then he warms me with his kind heart. We talk of the corn crop that needs to be picked but the ground has been too wet. He never cursed the rain and you could tell he has accepted the life of a farmer. In the distance, I see his son, the 45-year-old farmer who has finally found love. He met a woman who through life and pain has learned to look past the childhood images of white picket fences and daisies growing in the front yard. She saw a man covered in hog manure. But what she really saw was a kind heart that he got from his father and a purpose, direction, and devotion that came from his mother. I watch them as a silent observer and the memories they are forming are simple as they should be and will carry them on days when new memories become complex.

The prayer is said and the food is served. Aunt Kathy sits by my side and the joy of this feast to me is to be near her. I try to not examine the moment and just live in it. The questions I rehearsed in my head spin in search of an opening to be asked but I remain the silent observer. A painting that was done by Aunt Kathy many years ago hangs on the wall in this room. The painting is of Jesus and I ask Aunt Kathy about it. She tells me about the painting and all the other ones she did before the pitter-patter of the six children she had late in life. Her tired eyes dance with energy as she speaks of the paintings. From where I am sitting the painting of Jesus is above her head so it is easy for me to listen, look at her, and glance at the painting. For a moment, the chatter from everyone else is gone and I am immersed in the moment and her energy. She talks of the 15 years she was a Catholic nun and the things she loved to paint. She said, "I had to see what I was painting, I could not just make something up." I looked up at the painting of Jesus and I guess she saw him at some point or maybe she felt him. Her energy dropped off and the chatter returned but the moment will forever stay with me.

I went to the back of the truck and got my dog out of his crate. He needed to stretch his legs and I needed to further rehearse the questions I wanted to ask Aunt Kathy. We walked along the edge of the cornfield and I could see that the corn needed to be picked. The bright yellow kernels brought life to the brown, dried, withered corn stalks. Some of the ears of corn seem to be hanging on by a thread of life. We walked towards the creek and I recall about a year ago I stood here with Uncle Bill as the soybeans were being combined. In the last year and half I have come up with about any excuse you can imagine to make this trip, some 15 hours to this place. As if Aunt Kathy bears the answers that I so desire or the sky above this cornfield will open up and beam down my purpose for meeting her. My dog walks into the creek and drinks from that water that almost killed Uncle Bill many years ago.

His tractor turned over and he was pinned under the freezing cold waters with only his mouth able to get air. A boy who lived on the same gravel road as Aunt Kathy and Uncle Bill found him and went for help. The boy back then was unofficially classified as slow but no matter how you classified him now or back then, he was blessed with the power to help Uncle Bill.

I was tempted to throw rocks in the creek but I was afraid my dog would see that as an opportunity to get more than his feet wet. I could see the two houses in the distance and even though my dog was headed back up the road, I decided to walk around the cornfield. The deer had made a nice path around the edge of the cornfield and left evidence that ears of corn hanging on by a thread were part of their daily Thanksgiving feast. The deer, like Uncle Bill, have learned to accept the life of a farmer. I followed the muddy path the deer made and before I knew it, I made a loop around the cornfield. I could then hear the laughter of children playing in the back yard. As I got closer, I saw the second house and all I would have to do is just walk up to it but I decided to take another loop around the field. My dog, the smarter of this duo gives me a look and I correct him with "come on." We make it back to the creek and take the road to the first house. I find an old stump and sit there admiring the peace of the unpicked cornfield and the sky above.

There always seems to be an intersection in life not just the intersection that lies in front of me. There are choices to be made that require planning and other choices that must be made in a split second. My questions to Aunt Kathy are ones that have required planning on my part. I am told I have a gift as the silent observer of moments and time. I am told I'm able to transfer those silent observed moments into a written form so others can see them just like Aunt Kathy did when she used to paint. I paint in words those silent images to embrace your soul when you too hang by a thread as though you are that ear of corn. In a few days, I turn 50 and can leave behind the world of the gun and badge. I feel currently that the gift is not being effectively used as I carry the gun and badge. For me it never was about the gun and badge, it was about helping others find peace. In recent years, I feel I cannot even help others find peace anymore. My question to Aunt Kathy was simply how did she know it was time to leave the convent and serve her God in the same way but wear a different uniform? Did she sit on stump and overlook an intersection before she made that decision? Did she make a loop around a cornfield and follow the tracks of others or did she make her own path?

My dog was not as content with sitting at the intersection at the edge of the cornfield. We walked back to the second house and the chatter was still there. Aunt Kathy was sitting at the same table surrounded by those that love her. Some were ones she made and some like me have joined in her loop. The chatter moved outside for the annual football game. The grand kids, the parents, and those who have joined in on this loop proceeded to play. I gave Aunt Kathy my jacket and blanket and she sat on the porch. If only the chair she was in would rock, this would have been a perfect moment in time but I was sure her memory banks were flooding. My mom joined her and they sat and cheered for both teams. They reminded me of two mother hens cackling about something. I found myself under an oak tree older than anyone here and once again I became the silent observer. Aunt Kathy's daughter, who lives in this house was watching her two small children play in the dirt and fallen oak leaves. Though she has never spoken to me about it, I know of the car accident that almost killed her and did kill her friend. She survived to marry and have five kids. She, like the rest on this farm, has accepted this life.

I stood under my tree and debated joining the game but the need to capture this moment seemed to be more important. On the porch sat the girl in her wheel chair with that smile on her face even though she could not play. Her dad stood by her side never treating her like the girl who can only move one finger. The chatter from the game is loud but oh so refreshing with life and love. I can see the young love between the hog farmer and his girl. She just slapped his butt and my oldest son's eyes got bigger. My wife smiled and laughed as she went from the hospital professional to a girl on a hillside playing football. My thoughts are interrupted when the chatter of the game stopped and everyone was focused on the sky. The strong but weak voice of Aunt Kathy yells to the sky and points, "It's my Ben." A bald eagle flew above the hillside football field. Fifteen years ago after his funeral I saw a bald eagle and wrote about it in his story.

There is a term in this family that they all speak of; it's called "the loop". The loop is when this family embraces another. The loop requires you to load up in a truck, tour the 500-acre farm, maybe have a beer, but most importantly, the loop expresses that they have accepted you into their world. I knew things were serious when Aunt Kathy told me her hog famer son took his girl for a loop. The loop on this farm is filled with intersections, creeks, and yes an occasional cow pie.

At the age 30 and after 15 years of being surrounded by Catholic nuns, Aunt Kathy went on a loop. She once told me the decision made her have an ulcer but when it was time it was time. She chose the road that Uncle Bill stood on and further down that road was the pitter-patter of six children. I realize from where I am standing, if not for her loop none of this would be here. The oak tree that, like me, is a silent observer would be here but the grandkids, the parents, those that have joined in on this loop, and the houses would not be here. There would be no bald eagle named Ben and there would be no me. The game is over and the sun is starting to set. There is talk of the second meal on this Thanksgiving Day but our time here has passed. We load up and my questions were never asked. We pass the local airport that is now named after the bald eagle named Ben. The three-hour drive to my mom's is longer than normal and I have little to say. The classic country songs give my mind a break from all the silent observing but until my observations reach paper, it will swirl in my head like the cold waters around Uncle Bill that day in the creek.

I sat down days later to write Aunt Kathy a letter to ask her what I should do and my letter turned into this, a story from a silent observer. Even though this story may not answer my questions, it may answer yours. Maybe this story will explain how some of us see life and how some of us paint life. I will always question why Aunt Kathy's and my paths have crossed. Am I to help her or is she to help me? I told her a month ago I sometimes feel like I am her last student. I am learning from her so I can paint these words so you too can learn from her. There is no doubt she painted Jesus and I know she never saw him but she felt him. I think that gift is called faith and I am pretty sure we all need faith in God and life.

Almost 50 years ago a woman devoted to God choose to take a loop. At that time, some people were less than supportive. The uniform for Aunt Kathy changed but the devotion to God was the same. As she took her loop, she flooded the world and that hillside farm with that same devotion. In a sense, we are all on a loop but we all have different levels of devotion. Its crystal clear this family has not been spared the trauma and broken fences that life has but it does not seem to slow them down. A daughter who is lucky to be alive, a granddaughter who can only move one finger, a son who soars the sky, and the woman worn and torn from cancer who leads them by devotion. They all have accepted life for what it is. They can paint a picture and never see the images that they are painting. They can bow their heads and feel they are truly blessed. There will always be intersections in life and choices to be made. I am pretty sure if I were to ask Aunt Kathy my question, her response would still not answer my questions. A man I've never met but has been moved by my so-called gift texted me this morning. His text read, "Trust in Lord with all your heart and do not lean on your own understandings; in all your ways acknowledge him, and he will direct your path". I'm pretty sure Aunt Kathy's version of the above proverbs would read, "Trust in Lord with all your heart and do not lean on your own understandings; in all your ways acknowledge him, and he will direct your loop and watch out for the cow pies".

- WLV -

Jeff Mitchell & Wm. Josey Visnovske

Story 16

The Transition Man

The two-cylinder John Deere tractor sounded louder as I got closer to the barn. The mower I was pulling behind the tractor cut through the Johnson grass like a hot knife through butter. I was sure that the rear wheel of the mower had cleared the edge of the barn, but when I turned the steering wheel hard to the right, I heard the wheel hit the building. I shut the mower down and got off the tractor. I did not break the wheel, but one of the metal bars that held it in place was bent. The ride to the house from the barn was about 100 yards, but it seemed like five miles. Dad walked out of the garage and asked, "What's wrong?" With my head held low, I told dad the story and finished the story with, "I'm sorry." Dad asked, "Were you messing around or working?" I said, "Working." Dad said, "Accidents happen." Dad was a man of few words, but when he spoke, I had learned that I had better listen. Dad never spoke about his father, and when it came to his mother, his words were limited. Dad once said, "I never had a really good teacher when it came to being a father, so I'm doing the best that I can with you."

I backed the mower into the garage, dad grabbed the cutting torch and said, "We need to heat up the bent metal and get it back into shape." The flame from the cutting torch heated the metal and soon the heat consumed the paint on the bent metal. Dad grabbed a steel pry bar and started to bend the metal back into its original shape. As the steel cooled down Dad said, "Since we heated the metal up, we made it weaker, and now we need to weld in another piece of steel to make it strong again."

I stood there with my hands having nothing to do except watch Dad fix my mistake. I guess my hands spoke to him when he asked, "You wanna weld the piece of metal in?" The smile on my face gave him the answer faster than the air in my lungs did. Dad had taught me how to weld, so after a few words from him, I was joining two pieces of metal together. I walked over to the corner of the garage and grabbed a can of spray paint from the shelf. I knew Dad would want to paint the exposed heated metal to keep it from rusting. Dad asked, "You're not gonna prime the paint first?" The way he asked the question, I already knew the answer. Dad said, "I've always told you, if you're gonna do something, do it right. If you just spray paint the bare metal it will last for a while, but if it's primed first, it gives the paint something to stick to. Lots of folks like to make things look pretty but, I prefer to make things last."

Dad let me prime and then paint the metal. When I was done, he took the empty paint can, walked out of the garage and said, "Hand me that steel pry bar." He took the steel pry bar, poked a hole in the empty paint can, pulled out a marble, and handed it to me. He smiled, like he was a magician on the center stage, handed me a rag and said, "Wipe it clean." I took the rag, wiped the paint from the glass marble, and placed it in my pocket. I never understood the purpose of primer until that day in the garage. I never knew a glass marble lived inside the paint can and that its job, or part, was to keep the paint mixed together. I learned all that from a man who had very little to say and who learned how to be a father by trial and error.

I stood in the garage and loaded my Harley for my trip. I had not taken a long trip since my dad died, almost 7 years ago. During the six months I had commuted back and forth from my home to my home state, I wondered if riding the Harley would change the way I felt when I straddled the steel horse. The trips back and forth helped me to process the slow death of my father. In the seven years since his last breath, life has helped me to realize that I must go on.

My wife and boys stood there looking at me as I stuffed my saddlebags full of clothes and never said a word. I had a lump in my throat as that thought crossed my mind about whether or not this would be the last time I would see them and it made me want to stop. I have seen and felt enough, in my almost 50 years, to know there are no guarantees, just life. I have come to accept that there is a plan, but it may not be our plan. I have come to accept pain. I have come to accept the fear of the unknown and just like the mileage between doing our part in life and doing our job, I too must travel the roads that were never a part of my plan.

During the first few hours of the trip, the steel horse thundered under me and I relived every road since I was 16. A dose of modern reality hit when I passed a house where I had felt the pain, uncovered the fire debris, and did my best to clean them up before I placed them in a body bag. When I was 16, I never would have guessed that part of my job when I grew up would be "the guy" who cleaned them up and placed them in body bags. I must admit, the first time I cleaned one up and placed him in a body bag, my head spun for weeks. Over the years, I have somehow found honor in that part of my job, but I know most people wonder how I do it.

The further I got away from my house, the less the modern doses of reality hit me. Now, it's new memories being made, or old ones that sting less. At times, it's as though I am riding with those before me. I rode to say my good bye to Billy when he had his last ride. I think of dad, but the pain is less, and the strength to do my part, to be the primer of life, has never been stronger. As I mold and teach my boys, I realize the raw metal of life needs to last, not just look pretty. I realize that bent and broken are part of the plan, and it is our response, to the bent and broken, that is doing our part. As the mile markers passed by the steel horse, the marbles bounced around in my head; mixing the past, the present, and questioning where the plan would go next.

As the miles shorten to my destination, my body is tired, but tucked away in a small town, is a group of people waiting for me. Knowing that, keeps me going. They are waiting for the man who five years ago was a stranger, but now he is one of them. Death and debris brought us together and the primer of life bonded us. The interstate is behind me now. The two lane roads that wind and flatten between fields of crops tell me I am closer to the town where the debris is gone, but the mark of death still lingers.

As I get closer to the town, my emotions rise and I can feel another lump in my throat. Like the lump in my throat as I stood in my garage, I recall the chaos and horror from five years ago. I recall that thought when my feet took the first step into this town and I questioned why I had come here. Was this the plan? As the steel horse guided me to his house, like it was on autopilot, I felt calmness and the lump in my throat had disappeared. I lowered the kickstand and they appeared in the driveway, the husband and wife I had met five years ago. They are the same husband and wife who had both survived the horror that killed 15. I nicknamed the husband the Devil Dog, which is another name for a Marine. I smelled like the road, bugs, and everything else a thousand miles could stick to me, but it did not stop the hugs. We made our way into the living room and the last thing I wanted to do was sit down, but I did to be polite. I still felt the steel horse under me even though she was sitting in the driveway. The Devil Dog, who was also a man of few words, asked, "Normally you fly here, so why did you ride your bike this time?" I said, "I'm on vacation and this trip is on me." He just looked at me and lowered his head. I was not sure if he was disappointed that my work did not pay to send me back here or if he was just honored that I would pay for the trip myself. The streetlights started to dim and the town that time had forgotten prepared for bed. We found a place to eat that was still open and shared a meal together. It was just us plus the primer that holds us together.

I used to enjoy my stays in hotels, but now, after many years of staying in them, they are a constant reminder of nights that I am away from my wife, boys, and dog. I have learned that, sometimes, the plan that is not ours covers our hands in dirt, blood, and tears, and that sometimes, no amount of soap and water can wipe them clean. I wish I could've slept better, but I did not even after a hot shower. I felt like my body, mind, and soul were on overload from the 1000-mile ride. I called the Devil Dog and asked if they had anyone in their town that did massages. He said they did and would make me an appointment. The Devil Dog walked me to the door, as if I was his son, and introduced me to the massage woman his family uses.

She reminded me of a skeptical dog on a front porch that was glad to see you, but had a concern as to why you were there. I guess, from appearances, I appeared to have nothing wrong with me that would bring me to her door. I explained how I had ridden my Harley a thousand miles to come to the five-year anniversary, and how I had "jacked" a few things up on the ride. I think the skeptical dog left the room when she put her hands on my shoulders and felt the tight, knotted muscles. I could not see her face, but her voice changed, and her hands told me she sensed I was a friend, not foe. Over the next hour, I learned of her life and she learned of mine. She opened the muscle tissues so the blood would flow, and I am sure that I may have opened her heart a little, so that the skeptical dog would not be so skeptical. Just like the body naturally compensates for injuries, the brain does its best to naturally resolve the conflict (trauma) we take in through our five senses. The compensation and method to resolve the conflict is not always the best choice, but the body and brain only has so much to work with. The physical injuries are always so much easier to recognize than the emotional ones. I wondered if my trip here was about her, or the friends I came to see, or was this just about the time between the next plan?

The next few days consisted of what has become a routine over the last few years. The Devil Dog takes me around town like his son who just came back from somewhere. The Devil Dog's family embraces me and so do those who stood by his side that day the 15 left us. This year, I was blessed with the return of the City Girl, who had come to this place with me the first time. Over the years, since we first met here, we have become friends, and yes, the primer of life bonds us. The City Girl brought her husband. I had nicknamed the Reaper years ago. He was a man who had given much, then woke up one day with nothing left to take care of himself. Like many of us, his struggles are within, his paint can was empty, and he held a marble in one hand.

There is one here who holds my heart and not a day goes by where do I not think of her. Years ago, I had nicknamed her the Mother Hen and I am pretty sure the name needs no explaining. She reminds me of the mother hen who ran the chicken coop we had when I was growing up. She watches the door to the station, monitoring all who enter, to keep her boys safe. She puts everyone else before herself and when she has a thought about her own self, she feels guilty about it. Over the years, she has learned to trust me, but she still wonders if I will forget my way back to this little town.

As I entered the station, she saw me and knew that the stranger had found his way back home. The Mother Hen held me in her arms and said, "Thanks for coming." It was a hug that could only be described as one that comes from the depths of your soul; like greeting a loved one upon their return home after they had been gone for a long period of time.   Before I could catch my breath, the Mother Hen told me that the Dutchman had lost his quarter that I gave to him a few years ago. I said, "I have one in my pocket."   She dragged me over to the Dutchman, who towers over me in size. He hugged me, started to cry, and said, "I lost my quarter." I smiled and said, "Open your hand." The Dutchman opened his hands that are as big and worn as an old cast iron frying pan. I reached into my pocket, pulled out a one-shot quarter, and placed it in his hand. He grabbed it and attached it to his key ring, the same way he had attached it five years earlier when he told me his story of the night the 15 died. Once the quarter was on his key chain and his keys were back in his pocket, the gentle giant smiled down at me.

Before long, we were all loaded up and made our rounds to the cemeteries to see the 15 and the place where it happened. We walked around like we always do, in a state of confusion, with questions that linger above us as to why? I was not there that night, but somehow it felt like I was. I can see and feel the pain all around us. Every year, they seem to be better with this place.   Some have accepted the event and then accepted the outcome, but there are those who have still not accepted the outcome, and they seem to be stuck in time. I placed my arm around the Mother Hen and asked, "Does it feel like five years or five minutes?" She said, "It jumps back and forth and never stays in one spot very long." It's hard being there because I feel like I'm intruding on their holy ground, but a part of me has accepted this as part of my plan. I feel like I am to protect them from the outside world and in a sense explain to others what lies deep within this little town.

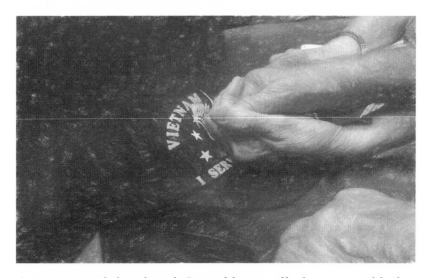

As we entered the chapel, I would normally have sat with the Mother Hen, but she directed me to sit with the Devil Dog. I reached into my pocket and handed him my collection of dog tags and religious medals. The first time he held them was five years ago and the collection has grown since then. Several dog tags have been added to it to include his. The Devil Dog held his wife's hand and in the middle was my collection of dog tags and medals. On the edge of his knee, in front of their hands, was his Vietnam Veteran hat. Several people spoke at the chapel, but I could not tell you one word that was said. I stared at the sight of their hands surrounding the collection and thought of those who have donated to that collection. I thought of the times I held that collection and felt the primer stick to my hands. I thought of the others who have held the collection as if it had magical powers. From the jungles of Vietnam, the desert of Iraq, the small private airstrip, the Hospice beds, a place called Waco, the cross from a hybrid nun, and the list goes on. The collection, to me, is a symbol of the primer of life. I smile when I recall how it all started with a young man who tried to show his father a magic trick by placing a bullet hole through a quarter at 100 yards. I suppose a feeble attempt to compete with a magic trick of getting a marble out of an empty paint can.

As we say, our goodbyes at the station, the Mother Hen will not sleep well until she knows I am home with my family. I told her I was sorry that I did not get to visit with her more. She smiled and said, "It's ok. I just need to know you are real." The Devil Dog and I rode back to his house where my steel horse awaited. Under his carport, the white Harley beckoned me that it was time to go home. The Devil Dog had little to say as usual and then the lump in my throat appeared with great force. I feel like I am back on that tractor and I have to tell my dad that I bent that steel. He parked in the driveway and I saw his wife look out of the window.

My hands are sweating and I am scared. I cleared my throat and said, "I've never asked you once about that night or Vietnam, but I got questions." He lowered his head, and in the dim lit driveway, I could see his face well enough that I could tell he was not mad. He said, "Ask your question." I said, "When we first met, you had just gotten out of the hospital and you had somehow survived what killed 15 people. I knew your life and town had been flipped upside down. You never spoke of that night, or of being in Vietnam, or of being a Marine. Now you wear your Marine or veteran hat everywhere you go and you seem to be proud to have served, where you did not seem proud before."

He lifted his head, took his hat from his head, and said, "I went over there to Vietnam and did what they told me to do. I did my job, but when I came home, I had no idea that my country would greet me like they did. I had no idea they would say what they said to us. When the 15 died, I was just doing my job. I woke up in a hospital and was told 15 died. People I knew my whole life were dead and they died next to me. People I was in charge of. I did nothing wrong, but I figured my country would once again shame me for doing my job. When I was not blamed or shamed for doing my job, I guess I got my faith back in my country and now I wear the hat everywhere I go. I had a duplicate dog tag made for each one of my grandkids because they need to know their grandpa served and was a Marine." For a man of few words, I sat there, and for once the plan seemed to make sense. I said, "So, if not for that horrible day, you would have spent the rest of your life with your head held low and Vietnam would have stayed tucked away inside of you?" The Devil Dog put his hat on, looked over at me, said, "Yes," and smiled like a magician on center stage. I am not sure if I just pointed something out to him, or if that was his way of thanking me, or if he just felt good to have served, and told a fellow Marine his very short story. No matter what the case, it was a hell of magic show and one I will never forget.

I used to help a friend train German Shepherds and my friend taught me a lot about dogs. When I became a father, I saw where kids and dogs have a lot in common. They both love routines and they both need to leave the training field confident and successful. He would always say, "Make sure the dog leaves the training field with their tail up and an extra bounce in their stride."

My routine in the morning includes a protein shake and stretching for a good hour. I have stretched for over 35 years. I guess there is this thing called Yoga, but I doubt that a guy who wears a belt buckle would tell the world he does Yoga, so I stretch. I had my protein shake in the hotel room and scanned the TV for something to watch while I stretched. The original TV series, The Lone Ranger, was on so I watched it. When I was a kid, I would watch The Lone Ranger, on a black and white TV, every morning while I ate the hot breakfast my mom had made for me. I then walked the ¼ mile to catch the school bus and dreamed of being The Lone Ranger when I grew up.

At daybreak, I loaded my saddlebags and started on my thousand-mile ride home. As I drove through that little town and passed the corn growing on the outskirts of town, tears found their way into the wind sliding by my face. In the mirror, I said good-bye to the little town I had nicknamed, the City of Hope, years ago. My visits here go much deeper than anniversary dates and my need to do my part. My visits here have the fuel stops I need, but gasoline is not the fuel I search for. The fuel that I run low on and search for is hope, it is here that I come to refuel. Hope that we as a society can survive the fast-paced, self-centered world it appears we have become. When I stop here in this town, I see the primer of life. I saw raw, bent and twisted metal, but now I see strong bonds between strangers that warm me on the coldest days.

My steel horse soon found its way to the interstate and mile markers told me that home was not that far away. I passed a shiny eighteen-wheeler tanker and saw my reflection in the shiny tank. My steel horse is white and then the message registered in my head, or two marbles just collided. I recalled last fall, a man interviewed me about that little town, and he was the first to inquire as to why I thought to give people a shot quarter or a shot key chain.

I hesitated with my answer and then explained that I had never told anyone about this before, to include the love of my life. I explained that when I lived with criminals, I was living out my childhood dream. I went to a town with a mask on, but in the end people knew I was good, then I disappeared into another town. I had become The Lone Ranger. I told the man about the day dad and I were in the backfield and he sat there in the wheelchair not feeling like a dad. The wheelchair was a result of cancer. I could tell he felt helpless. I could tell he felt there was no magic. Most of all I could feel his pain. I could not make it better, but I had the magic. I got behind my rifle, shot a hole through a quarter at 100 yards, and gave it to him. I now was the magician and I was on center stage. In that backfield, with a broken, bent, worn out man, I handed him hope in the form of a shot quarter. I gave my dad the primer of life. I'm not sure the man knew that would be the answer to his question, but it was the truth.

I guess to some it's childish and silly, but to me it's my silver bullet. In many ways, I still hide who I am, but never in the written words to you all. As I pass the shiny tanker, it's pretty clear, I'm still living out my child hood dream.

The steel horse thundered down the two lane black top road and the cotton plants growing in the field told me that my home was near. I saw the boys in the yard and it seemed like they had grown six inches. Their mother, who is the love of my life, stood there with a lump in her throat. Now she can rest. I'm home. I'm safe. I called the Mother Hen and told her that I was home and she said, "You should have broken the trip up." I said, "Love you too." My wife hugged me and I could feel her heart beat. Her mind had wondered for days, as the steel horse became my best friend. My wife used to ride behind me, but since the boys came along, she feels it's safer that one of us stays on the ground. My time on the steel horse causes her conflict, but she knows the steel horse has magic for me.

I too, suffer from the conflict of, "what if?" The phone rings at an odd time and the conflict begins. I formulate contingency plans, then the resolution, and then the perceived reaction to the conflict. I guess the reality of life has made me a contingency planner, or maybe God wired me that way, or truth be told I just don't want to be the guy with his head held low.

I spent the next few weeks processing that little town and all the things I have been blessed to be a part of. In the early morning hours, I found myself standing over several people who died in a fire. Once again, I had become "the guy" who cleaned them up and placed them in a body bag. As I did my job, and my part, I treated them as if they were my own. Once I was done, I walked out of the house, introduced myself to the family, and said, "I did my best and treated them like they were my own." I used to never introduce myself to the family, but in these situations, a mask is not needed. What is needed is compassion.

The woman who runs the karate school where I teach saw the fire on the news and asked if I had worked it? I told her I had. Normally, people say, "How do you do that job, it must be horrible." However, she said, "You, my friend, you are the Transition Man. You transition them from the place they died so they can get to a much better place. God will have a special place for you when your time comes." Her words were like a thousand marbles in my head. I take much honor and pride in doing a job that was not part of my plan, but most in society look at us cross-eyed when they know what we do.

I speak often of the plan and how most of us end up in a place we never thought we would. Since the words, Transition Man, bounced around in my head, I think we are all here to transition each other to a better place. Not just the dead, but also the living. We are all bent and bare metal at some point, but we all have the ability to give the primer of life. We have the power to heal, to soothe, and to knock the edge off whatever it is that ails us. There are times when there is no glass marble or silver bullet, but we are all blessed with the ability to show and feel compassion. Compassion seems to be needed more after the dust has settled and the headlines read of something else. We all get stuck in a spot in time. Some of us figure out how to the turn the page, but that one page is always bent over as if we have to come back to it, as if it has been marked. I feel it is our part to help each other transition through those bent and marked pages. The event does not have to be major, but it's major to whoever endured it. To be honest, I have no idea how we go about that. I do know that showing up and having compassion are a good place to start.

The Lone Ranger would show up and have compassion for those in need. He never wanted payment for helping and he never wanted credit for what he had done. My plan, back in the day, was simple; wear the mask, do good, and disappear into the hillsides. Now, my written words have been printed and people want to see the man behind the words. That is where my page gets bent or marked, but then I see the face of man who is stuck, and realize that in order to bring comfort and transition, we sometimes have to remove our mask.

As I type these words, a jar of glass marbles sits on the shelf. I have no idea which one was from dad, but it's in there. My collection of dog tags and medals sit on this desk to remind me that this may not be my plan, but it is my part in the primer of life. I hope these written words bring you comfort and I hope they have enough magic to transition you to a better place, or at least unbend that page that has you stuck.

- WLV –

Jeff Mitchell & Wm. Josey Visnovske

Marbles

"Life is pleasant. Death is peaceful. It's the transition that's troublesome."

> - Isaac Asimov (1920-1992) Professor of Biochemistry at Boston University, Science Fiction Writer, Author of over 500 books

Josey's dad was a good teacher for his son. He taught him that if he was going to do a job, he should always do it right. He taught him the importance of preparation before engaging in tasks. That always helped a job to be done right the first time. He made sure Josey used a primer on bare metal before applying paint. The primer acted as a bonding agent between the metal and the paint.

The word primer comes from a Latin word, 'primarius.' It means 'primary' or 'first.' (Sorry, I just can't help myself.) Knowing the derivation of a word gives us a much better understanding of how the word is used in modern English. In the ancient Latin, the word became associated with the term 'liber,' as in, 'primarius liber,' the 'first book.' We often hear the term primary school. Today primer refers to many things that prepare people for additional steps or activities. A primer may be used by women as a base coat for cosmetics. Primer can be a small pump that pumps some fuel into an internal combustion engine, such as an aircraft engine, to help start the engine. A primer is a substance used to prepare unpainted wood, metal, or canvas for the final coat of paint. It prevents the absorption of paint into the material, it chemically binds with the material as well the paint and helps it to stick and it prevents rust.

A family can be a life primer. Children become socialized within the family system. They learn to stick to the family members. If the parenting is good the children learn good things. They feel safe and they grow in self confidence and they learn sharing, kindness, generosity, concern, support, understanding, anger control, humor, loyalty, honesty, and a great many things that will help them to take on the responsibilities of adulthood such as a job, marriage, and family responsibilities.

On the other hand, if the parenting is absent or ineffective, the primer of life is no good. Children then learn insecurity, anger, bullying, cruelty, selfishness, complacency, rage, and revenge. They withdraw from responsibility; they look for the easy way to do things. They become takers not givers.

There is something else that is learned in families and that is the importance of rewarding behaviors. Rewards go much farther in developing emotionally healthy children than any form of punishment. Small rewards given by a parent to a child, particularly when the timing is right and the reward is deserved can have a powerful impact on a person's development. Parents also have an important role in helping growing children to recognize life rewards like the joy of properly completing a job, the value of a solid friendship or the feeling of pride and an elevated spirit that arises when helping a distressed person at a difficult time.

Life rewards are even recognized in the animal world. As one dog trainer noted, "You don't train a dog in a training hall, jerking his neck or even giving him food treats. You train him using life rewards."

> - Ian Dunbar (1947-) Veterinarian, Animal
> Behaviorist, Dog trainer.

The dog will recognize a friend and can reciprocate with loyalty and protection of the people in his world who have treated him with kindness.

Josey's family was not well off financially. They did, however, find ways to reward their children. When Josey's dad broke open the empty can of spray paint and smiled warmly at his son and gave him a glass mixing marble from the can, it touched Josey's heart. He still has that marble decades after he received it from his dad. He also learned how to reward his own children, other people he meets, and even his own dad. He amused and impressed and warmed the hearts of others by shooting holes in coins and Marine Corps key chains or giving people small plastic rabbits. It's all little things, but like Josey's marble, little things make people feel thought of, cared for, and warmed. The little gifts touched their hearts.

"The best and most beautiful things in the world cannot be seen or even touched - they must be felt with the heart."

> - Helen Keller, (1880- 1968) American author, political activist and lecturer. She was the first deaf and blind person to obtain a bachelor's degree.

Josey was nicknamed the 'transition man' by the lady at the marshal arts training center where he teaches and where his children learn their karate. It is a huge compliment. She made this compliment to him in reference to the work he did preparing fire fatalities for removal from the scene where they died. She saw him as the man who transitions dead people from the horrible, ugly scene of a deadly fire to a clean place where they can be prepared for a respectful burial.

Josey not only serves as a transition man for the fire fatalities he encounters in his work. He can also be thought of as a transition man who helps people from a dark and painful place after a shocking emotional trauma to a place in life where they can regain hope, learn from their tragedies, and restore their lives as they come to terms with their losses. Transition work is the work he did over several years with the survivors in the small town that suffered a terrible loss of friends and family members when everything went very wrong in an instant.

The life primer Josey's parents gave him helped him to stick to other people when they were down and struggling. He demonstrates this trait by his yearly visits to the town where 15 people died one evening. He developed friendships and cared for the people of the town and he gave out 'marbles' like his dad had done for him. His marbles, those little gifts that say, 'I understand and I care" are not really marbles. They are the plastic rabbits, the shot quarters, and the Marine Corp key chains with bullet holes in them. The Dutchman in the story was very distressed about losing his shot quarter that Josey had given him. Josey made his peace of mind return when he gave him a replacement shot quarter. A little 'marble', like his dad gave him at just the right time.

Life is often made up of 'marbles.' They can raise people's spirits in tough times when someone thinks about you, lets you know they understand and that they care. Be aware of marbles in your life. Give some; get some.

"Life is 10% what happens to you and 90% how you react to it."

> - Charles R. Swindoll, (1934-) Evangelical Christian Pastor and writer

- JTM –

About the Authors

William "Josey" L. Visnovske

William "Josey" Visnovske was born in the Midwest on a small farm to blue-collar parents. At an early age, he found the outdoors to be a place that he felt more connected to than the concrete and asphalt world that lies far away from their hillside farm.

Josey has been in law enforcement for over 28 years. He has served as a deputy sheriff, a city police officer, a state law enforcement officer, a federal agent, and a United States Marine. He is currently working as a certified fire investigator and a certified explosive specialist.

He is an International Critical Incident Stress Foundation approved instructor in ten categories. He also volunteers as a specialized peer support team member at the On Site Academy in Massachusetts; a residential training and treatment facility for emergency and military personnel struggling with critical incident stress and Post Traumatic Stress Disorder. During the last eight years, he has worked closely with Dr. Mitchell, conducting research and developing new concepts to the field of critical incidents.

At an early age, he was sent home from school for a three-day suspension. It was then he wrote his first story about the field behind his home. He soon realized that writing simply made him feel better, but it was not until he met Dr. Mitchell that he fully comprehended how writing was a way of coping and processing. When Dr. Mitchell suggested they write a book (Crucial Moments) he was very reluctant to share his personal writings with strangers, but he did. After the first book was published, and he received feedback that it helped people, he was glad that he did it. After a few more years of being himself and assisting people in critical incidents, he decided it was time for another book (Sister Mary, the Baker, the Barber, and the Brick Layer). In this book, he wanted to highlight and define the same recurring issues with most critical incidents. He dug deep inside of himself and exposed his own struggles in an effort to help the reader learn how to use self-care when a critical incident found its way into their backfields. After the second book was published, he once again received feedback that it helped people, so he decided to tackle another book. This book was written to stress the importance of having an internal self-care system. We have to make sure as we help others process the expected and the unexpected events of life that we take care of ourselves too.

Josey is a family man and his family is very involved with his work in critical incidents. He is a woodsman, an avid hunter, and the woods is where is writes his stories in his head. He has spent most of his life trying to fit in, but when he enters the woods, he feels he fits perfectly right there.

To this day, after years of writing, and three published books, he will tell you that he is not writer, but just a country boy who puts stuff on paper.

-WLV-

Jeffrey T Mitchell, Ph.D., CCISM

Jeffrey T. Mitchell, PhD is Clinical Professor of Emergency Health Services at the University of Maryland, Baltimore County, Maryland. He is a co-founder and President Emeritus of the International Critical Incident Stress Foundation. He holds a Ph.D. in Human Development from the University of Maryland. After serving as a firefighter/paramedic for ten years, he developed a comprehensive, integrated, systematic, and multi-component crisis intervention program called "Critical Incident Stress Management."

Dr. Mitchell has authored over 275 articles and 20 books in the stress and crisis intervention fields. He is an adjunct faculty member of the Emergency Management Institute of the Federal Emergency Management Agency. He is also a part time faculty member at Johns Hopkins University and he teaches the on-line Psychology of Disasters and the Crisis and Conflict resolution courses for the Florida Institute of Technology. He is a reviewer for the Journal of the American Medical Association as well as Disaster Medicine. He received the Austrian Red Cross Bronze Medal for his work in Crisis Intervention in the aftermath of the Kaprum Train tunnel fire. The Association of Traumatic Stress Specialists approved Dr. Mitchell as a Certified Trauma Specialist. The United Nations appointed him to the United Nations Department of Safety and Security Working Group on Stress.

- END -

Made in the USA
Columbia, SC
02 May 2019